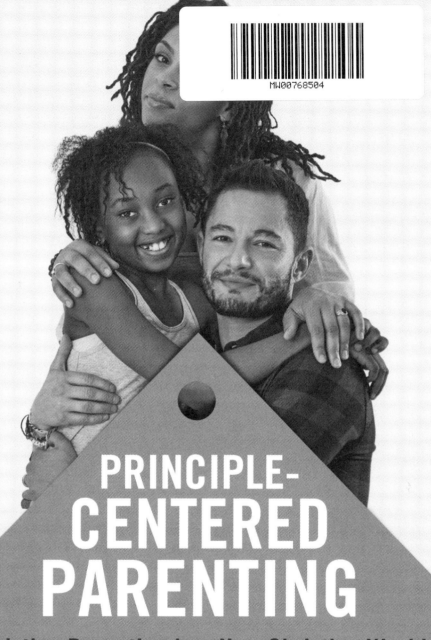

PRINCIPLE-CENTERED PARENTING

Christian Parenting in a Non-Christian World

DOUGLAS & VICKI JACOBY

Principle-Centered Parenting

*Christian Parenting
in a Non-Christian World*

Douglas and Vicki Jacoby

ILLUMINATION PUBLISHERS

PRINCIPLE-CENTERED PARENTING
Christian Parenting in a Non-Christian World
Revised Edition. © 2017 by Douglas and Vicki Jacoby
Original title: *The Quiver: Christian Parenting in a Non-Christian World* (2005)

Printed in the United States of America.

Interior layout: Toney C. Mulhollan. Cover design: Roy Applesamy.

ISBN 978-1-946800-67-1.

BIBLE VERSIONS CITED IN THIS BOOK
HCSB   Holman Christian Standard Bible
KJV   King James Version
NAB   New American Bible
NASB   New American Standard Bible
NIV   New International Version
NJB   New Jerusalem Bible
NKJV   New King James Version
NLT   New Living Translation
NRSV   New Revised Standard Version
TNIV   Today's New International Version

Illumination Publishers International
www.ipibooks.com
6010 Pinecreek Ridge Court
Spring, Texas 77379

*To our parents
and grandparents*

CONTENTS

I

First Things

Arrows in the Quiver

Like arrows in the hand of a warrior,
so are the children of one's youth.
How blessed is the man whose quiver is full of them.
(Psalm 127:3-5a NASB)

Psalm 127 is one of two psalms in the Bible penned by Solomon. In his analogy, the quiver holds the children—the quiver is the home. Although we don't frequently see them these days, quivers are simply portable containers for holding arrows. It is important to note that they are only *temporary* housings for the projectiles they carry.

To bring up children requires not only a "quiver," but also a "bow"—God's word. After all, can arrows be shot without a bow? The parents are the archers, who by skillful use of the bow launch the arrows. This requires a steady hand, a keen eye, and a calm spirit. Patience, not haste, is of the essence. The goal, of course, is not to maximize the number of arrows, or their velocity, but to hit the target. Yes, the Lord has something very specific in mind for us as parents. We dare not parent "at random."

Parenting Is Not Parentage

It speaks volumes that our society requires a license before one is permitted to drive a car, but not before one becomes a parent—an enterprise far more precarious and potentially life-threatening! In Britain and Australia, where we used to live,

I acquired my drivers' licenses only with considerable study and practice. (And that was years after becoming a licensed driver in the United States, where the standard is...well, let's just say that, in some countries, nearly anyone can pass the test. And in less scrupulous countries, you can virtually *buy* your license, if the price is right!)

Should the government issue parenting licenses? While we would vigorously resist such attempts at social engineering, such a policy would at least show that someone high up recognized that not everyone is qualified to parent. (And the same argument could be made for, say, marriage.) Unless we expect government to step in and encroach on yet another area of private life, we parents are going to have to do the right thing, use common sense, and take full responsibility for our families, not blaming unfortunate events on genes, the environment, the schools, or even the government.

First, as in any other field of human endeavor, parenting requires training. Grandparents and others from the previous generation are the logical choices for this. Second, good parenting entails practice. Granted that no one is going to be issuing parenting licenses anytime soon, what can we do to best prepare ourselves for the responsibility, privilege, and honor of parenting? We would argue that parents need to:

1. be exposed to the principles of parenting in Scripture (2 Timothy 3:15, 1:5);

2. form solid convictions in this vital arena of human existence, in order to counter secular currents that resist God's parenting principles; and

3. develop practical yet biblical strategies.

The Vanishing Art

Regrettably, parenting is a vanishing art. Many fathers effectively abandon their children; they give their best energies to career, and even when they are physically at home they may not be emotionally present. Often mothers are run so ragged with their own career expectations that they have scant emotional energy for their little ones. Or children may be farmed out to caregivers. Parents timidly pull the bowstring, shooting their "arrows"—but at what? Is there a clear target? God never meant for us to parent out of insecurity or fear, but that is what often happens. Too many parents fear failure, the disapproval of their relatives and neighbors, or the stern scrutiny of Social Services. Yet their greatest fear is that they will lose their relationship with their kids. "If I take a firm line, he/she may not love me anymore." It is hard to love people when fear gets in the way, and hard for them to reciprocate. And so, defaulting to the parenting style under which they themselves were brought up, moms and dads are caught in vicious cycles, unable to relate to their children as they wish to.

Sadly, many abdicate, relegating their kids to virtual video worlds, or relinquishing them to restless (sometimes lawless) friends. Yet deep down kids *want* us to give them direction. They need us to guide them, and deep down they know it. Failure to do so on our part constitutes a breach in our God-given responsibility. It also damages their sense of identity and security.

Children Need Their Parents!

Fortunately, the Bible contains numerous parenting principles; our job is to grasp and apply them to our situation. Unless we internalize these principles, we will ever be tempted to take shortcuts wherein "the end justifies the means," as we seek peace in the home and compliance from the kids. Above all, we must not abdicate. Only principle-centered parenting can save the next generation.

The experts tell us that most juvenile delinquents have been abandoned by their fathers and deprived of the affection they need from their mothers—as though we needed experts to tell us that! Quite simply, proper parenting is the answer to the majority of our social ills. The clear truth that emerges through the familial malaise of the last half century is this: *Children need their parents.* Narcissism is all about self-fulfillment; it conflicts with the self-sacrificing love of a good parent. As Paul wrote, *"After all, children should not have to save up for their parents, but parents for their children"* (2 Corinthians 12:14b). Self-centered parenting is the opposite of principle-centered parenting.

Principle-Centered Parenting

We are a family of five—with one son and two daughters, now grown—and we love being parents. We certainly don't claim to be the ideal family, but we're striving to live by the principles of God's word, and we are very proud of all our children. Principles are not methods, gimmicks, or battle tactics. They are eternal truths, and they are in the Bible. Like all principles, they must be applied with wisdom.

Our aim in this book isn't to get you to do things "our way." After all, we have made mistakes in our parenting over the years! Yet we're completely convinced that, when it comes to building family, God has the answers, even if we don't.

In short, this is a book about biblical *principles*. As you read, please keep in mind a few things. First, we take it for granted that you have at least one child and love him/her. If you aren't a parent (yet), you may benefit from the book, but it is written primarily for mothers and fathers. Next, we're pretty sure that you believe in the Scriptures as the word of God—or at least are willing to look there for answers as you parent your child/children. This is vital, because hundreds of parenting books have been written—many of them highly recommendable—yet the only authoritative "text" is the Bible. We also trust that you're willing to sacrifice some things in your life in order to build family—in other words, to reprioritize. You're willing to pay the price; you aren't looking for shortcuts. That's good, because God's word doesn't offer any.

We believe this book will help you prepare your children for their future by imparting to them biblical convictions and a biblical worldview. Further, it will clarify the boundaries of parental accountability, calling you to mature and complete responsibility while setting you free from unhealthy self-imposed restrictions. In short, our prayer is that this book will equip you to launch those arrows!

God's Children

For "In him we live and move and have our being"; as even some
of your own poets have said, "For we too are his offspring" (Acts
17:28 NRS).

Has not the LORD made them one? In flesh and spirit they are
his. And why one? Because he was seeking godly offspring...
(Malachi 2:15 NIV) .

All people are God's children in one sense (Acts 17:28), yet
his heart's desire is to have *godly* offspring—godly family
(Malachi 2:15). Only the man Jesus Christ perfectly fulfilled
that ideal, yet we have an opportunity to become God's sons
and daughters in a special way when we become Christians
(John 1:12–13).

In 1 Timothy 2:3–4 we read that God our Savior *"wants
everyone to be saved and to come to the knowledge of the truth"*
(NASB). Though it is God's will that every person be saved,
not all do become Christians. It is important to remember
that the Lord doesn't force anyone to follow him. He respects
their freewill choices. Although this is hard for us as parents—
staying calm even when our children make wrong decisions—
it is part of being godly mothers and fathers.

Parenting and Family

If God is, generally speaking, the Father of all mankind, it
should be pretty obvious that parenting and creating family
are not the same thing. Most people can procreate or adopt

children—that is, become parents—but that is not the same thing as building family.

Family entails relationship, love, forgiveness, safety, nurture, growth, and so much more. Most people concede that their family life is far from ideal, but few truly turn to God for the guidance so sorely needed. Wise parents look to their Creator, their own heavenly Father. *really, with the only answer? No, def. not the best answer!!*

Character Counts

turned

Since God is the perfect parent, we should imitate him to the best of our ability. That includes aiming to have "godly offspring." Are we willing to ask ourselves, what words describe my family? What would outsiders say? "Wealthy, educated, and out of control"? Or maybe "quiet, reserved, and focused"? Would "godly" be one of the words they would use to describe your family? *Nope*

"Godly" doesn't suggest religious activity as much as *character*. It means we, and our children, should try to be "imitators of God," and especially "live a life of love" (Ephesians 5:1). Character is not easily acquired; it is built by persevering through hardship. *"We also rejoice in our sufferings, because we know that suffering produces perseverance; perseverance, character; and character, hope"* (Romans 5:3–4). It takes work. Character counts.

The Bible Has the Answers

Our philosophy of parenting is that the Bible has the answers. Somewhere in the Scriptures is the answer to my question, the solution to my problem. We need to search for those answers, and then put them into practice. The wisdom of the Bible—the principles revealed by God for creating family—was intended to be public information, even though most people among the public haven't benefited from it. The Scriptures are truly worth their weight in gold. The Bible recounts the lives, and family lives, of many people. We study their lives to see their godly (and sometimes ungodly) qualities and learn from them, so that we may find solutions based on biblical principles. Interactive discussions with other godly parents will spark lots of ideas, and is certainly valuable, but only digging deeper for conviction from the Scriptures will make us as parents "hold to the truth" and not just try another angle, a different tack.

Children know if we are convinced from the Scriptures or if we are trying out a shortcut, a "new" approach. They can tell whether Mom and Dad just got off the phone from getting advice from other Christians or whether their convictions really come from the Bible.

Practicals or Principles?

It's important to resist the temptation to jump to the practicals before we have internalized the principles. Principles stand the test of time, but how we implement them will change as the world we live in changes. So will circumstances. Moreover, each child is different, as is every household, generation, and culture.

Our family has lived on three continents and visited scores of nations. We have seen that the truths of God's word apply in *all* settings and cultures. This, for us, is powerful evidence that the Bible contains the truth and can be fully trusted as our guide and compass in all areas of life, including parenting.

The Goal

We have seen that the real goal of parenting is *to raise godly offspring.* For some of us, however, it may feel as though the goal is to survive—just to make it through. If this is the case, take a deep breath and relax. Be encouraged. There are real answers in the Scriptures. For others, however, although things may be going smoothly enough, there is no real plan. You don't so much need encouragement as to hear the alarm. We cannot take such a casual approach to parenting.

For most of us, we hope to make the children happy, to give them a "better life" than we had. But this is insufficient, because it does not address their spiritual side. Even aiming to lead the kids to become Christians can—and often does— fall short. Raising godly offspring is more than converting our kids. It involves building family, training and equipping children for life, and preparing them to be launched into the adult world and to stand on their own feet before God. Part of this training is teaching them what family is and how to build it. Without training, don't we all naturally "default" to the sort of parenting style we were brought up with? (Strict, loose, tense, casual, messy, regimented, expressive, cool...)

But Will They Comply?

The children will not accept all that you try to teach them. Just as we resisted some of our own parents' input, our children, too, may prove rather selective in the bits of advice they decide to take. Don't worry; the purpose is not to make them become like you. Children cannot, will not, and must not be carbon copies of their parents. Living our life through our children—perhaps trying to compensate for insecurities and our own adolescent hang-ups—is a mark of immaturity. We must launch our children, but that means we must also release them. How can they become their own persons if we're still clinging to them?

Maturity means the ability to make one's own decisions— even wrong ones, like not following Christ. Now, it is certainly not wrong to do all one can to influence one's children to make a faith decision. But it is inconsistent to respect their free will *and* to accept only one response to the gospel. That sort of love would be based on performance, wouldn't it?

They must be free to say no, no to you and—are you surprised?—no to God. That is what freedom is, and that is the freedom he gave the first humans. He did not overpower them. This also means that you aren't a failure just because a child isn't following Christ.

Just Going through the Motions?

How easy it is for all of us, and especially "Christian kids," to just go through the motions. And how many times we see the children we love end up becoming "good people"—just like the Rich Young Ruler. For parents, Mark 10 must be one of the most haunting passages in the New Testament. The young man seems to have it all together, doesn't he? But his heart is not there—and God wanted his heart. Anyway, let's read the passage:

> [17]As Jesus started on his way, a man ran up to him and fell on his knees before him. "Good teacher," he asked, "what must I do to inherit eternal life?"
>
> [18]"Why do you call me good?" Jesus answered. "No one is good—except God alone. [19]You know the commandments: 'Do not murder, do not commit adultery, do not steal, do not give false testimony, do not defraud, honor your father and mother.'"
>
> [20]"Teacher," he declared, "all these I have kept since I was a boy."
>
> [21]Jesus looked at him and loved him. "One thing you lack," he said. "Go, sell everything you have and give to the poor, and you will have treasure in heaven. Then come, follow me."
>
> [22]At this the man's face fell. He went away sad, because he had great wealth (Mark 10:17–22).

This young man had probably been brought up in a "good home." His sins were not egregious. He was a nice guy—like all the other "nice people" out there. Yet he was unwilling to take a stand when called upon to put God first. He may have believed in God and the Scriptures, but he couldn't bring himself to submit his priorities to Jesus Christ. Perhaps his parents had provided him with a "better life" than they had, and he had become too comfortable with it—as in many families today.

Jesus did not chase after him. Although obviously the Lord disagreed with the young man's decision, he refused to force himself on him, although it was well within his power. Nor did Jesus shift the blame to the man's parents. No, this man stood before God on his own two feet, and Jesus allowed him the freedom to choose.

Are you afraid this could happen to your children—that they might just go through the motions without having a real heart for God? We are. We all know from our own adult experience how easy it is to pretend to be happy, to fake being joyful Christians. Lord forbid that our children should lose touch with what they really think and feel, and so be tempted to merely play the game.

Or consider Luke 15:11–32, the well-known Parable of

the Lost Son. Interestingly, it is the *prodigal* son who has the clearer perspective on his father, not his more dutiful older brother. The older brother, ironically, turns out to be the "lost" one, the one going through the motions. Perhaps more significant, the father amazingly not only allowed his son to make an extremely poor decision, but also showed no trace of condemnation or judgmentalism when the prodigal returned home.

Conclusion

The goal is to launch our children. And yet they are only in the home for a short period of time—eighteen or twenty years, perhaps. The clock is ticking. We will do our best to point them in the right direction, and more often than not, parents who bring their children up in the instruction of the Lord "hit the target." But this is not a given. Not all children opt to follow in the footsteps of their parents. Perhaps a child will be converted, then wander from the faith, only to return years later. Or perhaps the child will never come back—at least not in the lifetime of the parent. Unconditional love demands that we respect the free will of our children, even when they use it to make a bad decision. For that is how our heavenly Father treats us, is it not?

"Godly offspring" (Malachi 2:15) implies character. We are convinced that if we focus on character, and on the heart, we will do far better at the end of the day than if we focus only on educating the kids, befriending them, or even on converting them.

The Rest of the Book

The book is divided into sections: First Things—which you have just finished—Family, Parents, Children, Rhythms, and Values. In the next section, "Family," we'll broaden our discussion of the importance of creating family. Family isn't automatic, nor does it just happen as soon as a child is born. (Just as a house is not necessarily a home.) What can we learn from the Bible about how to ensure that we are building real family?

II

Family

A Safe Haven

Some went out on the sea in ships…
He spoke and stirred up a tempest
    that lifted high the waves.
They mounted up to the heavens and went down to the
depths;
    in their peril their courage melted away…
Then they cried out to the LORD in their trouble,
    and he brought them out of their distress.
²He stilled the storm to a whisper;
    the waves of the sea were hushed.
They were glad when it grew calm,
    and he guided them to their desired haven.
                         (Psalm 107:23–30)

Thoughts from Douglas

    When it comes to family life, there is a lot going on! Sometimes the seas are rough, the weather stormy. The home is the refuge to which parents—and especially children—can turn for protection. We all need a "safe place"—a place to be ourselves, to relax, to speak freely, to be alone. We need a haven.

    In weddings I (Douglas) regularly heard the minister encourage the couple to make their home a "haven." So when I started performing weddings myself, I too used this language. But what exactly is a haven? I thought I had better look it up.

    Originally, "haven" is a sailor's term. In fact, it appears in the English Bible in Genesis 49:13, Psalm 107:30 (quoted above), and Acts 27:8, all in nautical contexts. *The Oxford English Dictionary* entry is as follows:

> **Haven** (hēi·vʹn), sb. [Late OE. *hæfen, hæfne* (XI) – ON. *hofn (hafn)*,
> gen. *hafnar* = MLG., MDu. *havene*, Du. *haven* (whence G. *hafen*).] A
> recess or inlet of the sea, or the mouth of a river, affording good
> anchorage and a safe station for ships; a harbour, port. 2. *fig.* A
> refuge; an asylum ME.

I like that definition. It makes sense. Home should be peaceful, a place where the family finds protection from the evil in the world. Vicki and I have striven to make our home a safe place for the children, and also a fun place. The fun, I think, comes from Vicki. She loves to laugh, and she is a tremendous mother. I freely admit that her EQ (emotional intelligence) is many points higher than mine. Usually she is the one who draws out the children when they need to talk. She also helps me be a better communicator, and our twenty-five years of marriage have enticed me to come out of my shell and enjoy the party. As a result, the children not only love being with one another, but they also love coming home. It saddens us when we see so many children who don't get along with one another and can't wait to leave the nest. Sure, we believe in launching the kids, and in some ways I looked forward to the "empty nest" (what a profusion of metaphors!) and more time with my wife. But we love being with them, and we think that if anything has gone right in our home, the credit must go to God, who has given us so many parenting principles in his word.

Thoughts from Vicki

Just as the church is the body of Christ—the people and not the building—our homes are the members of our family. Family is our most treasured earthly possession. No one is more deeply connected to us than our children. They are our pride and joy, and God has entrusted us with them. Each child is a precious gift, one that loves and interacts with us, eager with expectation to experience life.

Before we can launch the kids, we must shelter them, protect them, and nurture them. The more children we have, the greater the need for the quiver to keep them all together and heading in the same direction. Many of us spend a lot of time on our houses, and we purchase or rent the right place near good schools or in a safe district to provide our kids every possible opportunity. Is the house more important than the occupants, who make the real home? It is easier to fix up the house than to create a home, a family that loves God.

Deep in our hearts we all crave a secure, loving, peaceful family where there is laughter and friendship. Nothing beats the picture of a family all together, including the grandparents, enjoying one another's company. It does not just happen. This picture has to be purposefully fashioned—a home, a haven.

What is your picture of a happy family? Perhaps it comes from a movie or a television series (*The Waltons, Little House on the Prairie, Leave It to Beaver, The Partridge Family, The Brady Bunch,* or—more concerning—*The Simpsons*). Maybe you have some great childhood memories or recall glimpses of other families you admired. It may be a special memory involving one of your grandparents. You want to create a secure environment like that in your own home.

I grew up in England, and not in a churchgoing family. My twin sisters are two years younger than I, and I have many happy, fun memories with them. Since we are not far apart in age, during our elementary years we were close; we were each other's best friends. As we went through the teenage years, however, we grew apart as each of us was consumed with making her own way, and we did less together as a family. Soon we went off to college, converging on home only for Christmas.

When I was twenty-four, my father was diagnosed with cancer; he died sixteen months later. This sad event not only renewed and strengthened our family ties, but also made me think a lot about creating family. My desire has been for our children to be great friends. I have expected it, I have prayed about it, and we have worked towards having tight relationships among them (no bickering, cutting remarks, sarcasm, or "silent treatment"). We have also tried to get all three to look out for one another. As 1 Corinthians 13:7 has it, love "always protects."

I have always wanted everyone to enjoy today together, as tomorrow is not a given.

Our upbringing affects our view of the ideal home, and yet, without a plan—an intentional direction and desire—we will probably revert to our default setting and do to our children what was done to us. We can create a haven only if we purposefully use our gifts and plan and pray to provide a godly environment. Such an environment is depicted by the fruit of the Spirit (Galatians 5:22–23), and such a family consists not in the impressive construction of the house, but in the spiritual atmosphere that overflows out of our hearts.

I always wanted a happy, fun, *relaxed* home. Douglas has always valued an *orderly* home. These two concepts have sometimes been in competition through the years (formal versus informal, cleaning versus relaxing), and the two of us have had many discussions. Yet both ideals—the happy home and the orderly home—bring security, although in different ways. After all, it is hard to be relaxed amid chaos. Similarly, order without unconditional acceptance does not make for a happy home. I am reminded of the von Trapp family in *The Sound of Music.* Maria was the spontaneous one; the baron was sterner. We have often laughed and cried as we watched the film and noted the similarities to our own family (who, by the way, also like to sing).

Finally, I believe that Mom is the key person in creating the right atmosphere: a nurturing environment, a nursery where flowers bloom and grow. Motherhood is a gift from God and is essential to making the home a haven.

Conclusion

What sort of home atmosphere do you want to work towards? Does your family need to "lighten up," "liven up," or "tighten up"? Change is best effected in an environment of security, because stress reduces our capacity to hope, to be flexible, and to hear one another. That is why it is so important that the home is a safe haven.

We will have to be intentional with our parenting if we and our children are to enjoy this quality of home life. That means resisting the negative influences of our society (Chapter 4) and making sure our relationships are in their proper biblical order (Chapter 5).

Family First!

They kept bringing pressure on Lot and moved forward to break down the door (Genesis 19:9b NIV).

We all agree that family should come first, yet this is easier said than done. Creating family is sometimes exhilarating or deeply satisfying, but the work is emotionally taxing and at times profoundly confusing.

Two men met at a bus stop and struck up a conversation. One of them kept complaining of family problems.

Finally, the other man said, "You think you have family problems? Listen to my situation. A few years ago I met a young widow with a grown-up daughter, and we got married. Later my father married my stepdaughter. That made my stepdaughter my stepmother and my father became my stepson. Also, my wife became mother-in-law of her father-in-law.

"Then the daughter of my wife, my stepmother, had a son. This boy was my half-brother because he was my father's son, but he was also the son of my wife's daughter, which made him my wife's grandson. That made me the grandfather of my half-brother.

"This was nothing until my wife and I had a son. Now the half-sister of my son, my stepmother, is also the grandmother. This makes my father the brother-in-law of my child, whose stepsister is my father's wife. I'm my stepmother's brother-in-law, my wife is her own child's aunt, my son is my father's nephew and I'm my own grandfather!

"And you think you have family problems!"

Hopefully the basics of family will be easier to understand than the humorous (and fictitious) story above! Still, it may be more difficult than we think. That is because when we try to take a step in a godly direction, the adversary pushes back. The world exerts considerable pressure and resists any attempt to stand our ground, let alone take steps in a positive direction.

Pounding Down the Door
The society of Sodom brought pressure on the household of Lot four thousand years ago, and things are no different today.

> [1]The two angels came to Sodom in the evening, and Lot was sitting in the gateway of Sodom. When Lot saw them, he rose to meet them, and bowed down with his face to the ground. [2]He said, "Please, my lords, turn aside to your servant's house and spend the night, and wash your feet; then you can rise early and go on your way." They said, "No; we will spend the night in the square." [3]But he urged them strongly; so they turned aside to him and entered his house; and he made them a feast….
>
> [4]But before they lay down, the men of the city, the men of Sodom, both young and old—all the people to the last man—surrounded the house; [5]and they called to Lot, "Where are the men who came to you tonight? Bring them out to us, so that we may know them" (Genesis 19:1–5).

Lot refuses to accede to their request, but (shockingly) offers his daughter to his fellow townsmen. But the Sodomites inis on their way.

> [9]But they replied, "Stand back!" And they said, "This fellow came here as an alien, and he would play the judge! Now we will deal worse with you than with them."
>
> Then they pressed hard against the man Lot, and came near the door to break it down. [10]But the men inside reached out their hands and brought Lot into the house with them, and shut the door (Genesis 19:9–10 NRSV).

What an abominable situation! If you want to see what would have likely happened to their guests, read what happened in a similar incident 800 years later:

¹[The Levite] went in and sat down in the open square of [Gibeah], but no one took them in to spend the night.
¹⁶Then at evening there was an old man coming from his work in the field… ¹⁷When the old man looked up and saw the wayfarer in the open square of the city, he said, "Where are you going and where do you come from?" ¹⁸He answered him, "We are passing from Bethlehem in Judah to the remote parts of the hill country of Ephraim, from which I come. I went to Bethlehem in Judah; and I am going to my home. Nobody has offered to take me in."
²⁰The old man said, "Peace be to you. I will care for all your wants; only do not spend the night in the square." ²¹So he brought him into his house, and fed the donkeys; they washed their feet, and ate and drank (Judges 19:15–21 NRSV).

And now history repeats itself:

²²The men of the city, a perverse lot, surrounded the house, and started pounding on the door. They said to the old man, the master of the house, "Bring out the man who came into your house, so that we may have intercourse with him."
²³And the man, the master of the house, went out to them and said to them, "No, my brothers, do not act so wickedly. Since this man is my guest, do not do this vile thing. ²⁴Here are my virgin daughter and his concubine; let me bring them out now. Ravish them and do whatever you want to them; but against this man do not do such a vile thing." ²⁵But the men would not listen to him (Judges 19:22–25a NRSV).

What comes next is hard to believe took place among the old covenant people of God.

So the man seized his concubine, and put her out to them. They wantonly raped her, and abused her all through the night until the morning. And as the dawn began to break, they let her go. ²⁶As morning appeared, the woman came and fell down at the door of the man's house where her master was, until it was light.
²⁷In the morning her master got up, opened the doors of the house, and when he went out to go on his way, there

was his concubine lying at the door of the house, with her hands on the threshold. [28a]"Get up," he said to her, "we are going." But there was no answer… (Judges 19:25b–28a NRSV).

The Ugly Truth

The Bible does not recount the story of the Levite and his concubine (secondary wife) so that we may imitate what we see. It recounts the lurid tale to illustrate how bad things were in Israel when God was not the true king (Judges 17:6, 18:1, 19:1, 21:25). Many horrific stories we see on the evening news are no worse. In fact, such happenings are absolutely *normal* when God is not honored in our society.

Ugly events like those related in Genesis are not only the experience of those who do not know God. Lot, despite his various and well-known compromises, was still considered a righteous man in the Bible (2 Peter 2:8). Righteous parents do not always succeed in protecting their families from the world. To be honest, we know a number of committed Christians whose families have at one time or another experienced woes of equal magnitude and heartbreak: drug and alcohol addictions, sexual sin, divorce, trouble with the law, and so forth.

The story of Lot is not included in the Bible so that we can look down on him. If anything, it is there as a warning to us (1 Corinthians 10:11) and as a reminder that, "There, but for the grace of God, go I."

Lessons Learned

Many lessons emerge from the gloomy tale of Lot's family in Sodom. We encourage you to study about his life (in Genesis) at greater length, though we will not develop the story any further here. Some observations:

- Even a God-fearing family can compromise with the world. (Lot's daughters were engaged to nonbelievers.) And this man was the relative of Abraham, the man of faith!

- Lot went for the easy way, compared with Abraham (see Genesis 13:10). He was as close to the world as you could possibly get. And yet didn't our Lord teach that God's people "are not of the world"? (John 17:14).

- He would not accept help or take advice. And even after he was rescued from destruction, he still didn't "get it" (Genesis 19:16, 18–20). His judgment had been tainted.

- The world tends to view people as objects and sources of pleasure or profit. Notice their attitude towards the old man's guests and also the absence of hospitality in their city. This view—considering others as objects—eventually infects young and old alike.

- Accordingly, the world brings strong pressure against the institution of the family. (This is becoming increasingly evident in modern Western society.)

- In keeping with the social conventions of the day, Lot was willing to place relations with outsiders (the undercover angels) above his own family.

- He failed to protect his daughters, and yet surely a father's duty is to protect his children—and especially daughters.

- God does not excuse such compromise. Sometimes, through the help of strong spiritual friends, he saves us from our own destructive behaviors.

Pressure!

Yes, the world constantly pressures us and our children in many ways, and not just sexually. It pressures us to:

- Spend money we don't have and buy things we don't need.

- Try to impress others rather than being real and vulnerable.

- Pour our lives into careers so that we may become "successful" and wealthy, rather than into relationships that count.

- Accept its "values" (what an oxymoron!) rather than putting God first.

This pressure comes through acquaintances, society at large, the media, business, and educational institutions. Worldly culture is highly corrosive. It tends to disintegrate—literally, "pull apart"—family life. This is such a significant danger that later in the book two complete chapters will be devoted to exploring it further.

Conclusion

Are we living near Sodom? We cannot escape the world (1 Corinthians 5:10), but we can prevent it from entering the doors of our heart. We must not love the world (1 John 2:15–17; James 4:4), or we are in effect inviting it into our lives and our family life. Rather, to refer to another personality from Genesis, we must be like Noah, who took a stand, obeyed God, and together with his sons persevered through faith and built the ark (Genesis 6–7). This righteous man walked with God and was "blameless among the people of his time" (Genesis 6:9), even though at that time "the earth was corrupt in God's sight and was full of violence" (Genesis 6:11). In contrast to Lot, Noah led his entire family to salvation. No one "looked back" (Genesis 19:26; see also Luke 17:32). Apparently, no one wanted to!

And yet, making our homes a safe haven requires more than just tuning out the bad influences of the world. We will be swimming upstream, resisting culture, and learning to say no to others when their appeals are not godly. We also need to understand the divine "ladder" of relationship priorities, and then adjust anything in our lives that works against that order.

The Ladder of Priorities

And whoever does not provide for relatives, and especially for family members, has denied the faith and is worse than an unbeliever (1 Timothy 5:8 NRSV).

In the last chapter we urged parents to resist the worldly pressures bearing down on the doors of our homes. In this chapter, we'll explore the relational framework that makes such resistance possible. We hope this study will transform the way you think about family!

The pressures of the world seek out structural weaknesses in our homes. Misplaced priorities constitute a structural weakness. Where there is structural weakness, there is the potential for collapse. Much of the collapse of the modern family would be avoided if we all respected what God's word says about relational priorities.

To help you think about the subject, please go through the following short exercise. Take a moment to reflect on your most important relationships. Consider the following: husband or wife, children, the church, the lost (those who do not yet know God), and of course the Lord. Arrange them into their order of importance—that is, starting with the most significant relationship. (Single parents, in this exercise, for simplicity, do not include your former spouse/partner.) In terms of your God-given Christian responsibility, list which one feels most important, second in importance, and so on.

1. _____
2. _____
3. _____
4. _____
5. _____

It may come as a surprise to some that there actually is a divine order of relationships. Did we perhaps think that all relationships are equally important, apart from our relationship with God? They aren't.

Divine Order

We harm our families, and the church family, when we disregard God's wisdom by which he set up his divine sequence. Let's begin with what we all agree, on paper at least, to be our most important relationship. We are pretty confident that you placed the Lord in the number one position. And this is right:

> [4]Hear, O Israel: The LORD our God, the LORD is one. [5]Love the LORD your God with all your heart and with all your soul and with all your strength (Deuteronomy 6:4–5).

If we love him with all our heart, there can be no one we love more. Both testaments agree that the Lord God is to be the ultimate recipient of our love and devotion. (In the New Testament, see Matthew 22:37, Mark 12:30, and Luke 10:27.) But are we really loving God with our whole heart? And do our children see us putting God first? Don't think they aren't watching. They know whether their father and mother really believe what they claim to profess at church. The kids know what we really love most.

In our family there are frequent discussions about the Lord. We talk about answered prayers, doors that he is opening (or closing), and how our faith is helping us through the day. We even talk about doubts—like: "In the light of so many tragic world events, how can we believe God is fair?" And we talk about the Bible, emphasizing that God's word holds the answers to all our most important questions. As far back as they can remember, our children have been taught the Scriptures. As Paul wrote in his last letter (before his execution):

> [14]But you must remain faithful to the things you have been taught. You know they are true, for you know you can trust those who taught you. [15]You have been taught the holy Scriptures from childhood, and they have given you the wisdom to receive the salvation that comes by trusting in Christ Jesus. [16]All Scripture is inspired by God and is useful to teach us what is true and to make us realize what is wrong in our lives. It straightens us out and teaches us to do what is right. [17]It is God's way of preparing us in every way, fully equipped for every good thing God wants us to do (2 Timothy 3:14–17, NLT).

Children taught the Scriptures, not only through verbal instruction but through the instruction that is "worth a thousand words," grow up wiser and better prepared for life. This is not because their parents are smarter than everybody else. Anything they do that's right is because they have discovered God's wisdom. It is neither likely nor realistic that we will have a close walk with God if we do not spend regular time in the word of God and in private prayer. For example, passages on putting the Word into our hearts include Joshua 1:8, Colossians 3:16, and 1 Timothy 4:16. Passages on prayer include Psalms 42:2, Ephesians 6:18, and 1 Thessalonians 5:17.

Our personal habits have a profound effect on the kids. Men, are you reading the Word and spending time in prayer? Or have other things crowded that out?

I (Vicki) would like to emphasize how important it is for the family that the husband puts God first. It gives me great security to know Douglas is spending time reading the Bible every day, as he has ever since I have known him. And it especially gives me encouragement to know that he is out walking and praying. It is so much easier to trust my husband when I know he is trusting in the Lord. I also really appreciate it when we go for a prayer walk together in the neighborhood.

Clearly, God comes first, according to Scripture, and this has big implications for how we spend our time. Failure of husband or wife (more typically the husband) to actively seek the Lord has a detrimental effect on the children. How can the family be godly if the leader of the family is taking them in an ungodly direction? (Luke 6:39). Yes, the Lord is first, and others second:

> [39]Love your neighbor as yourself (Leviticus 19:18b—also Matt. 5:43, 19:19, 22:39; Romans 13:9; Galatians 5:14; James 2:8).

Our neighbor, our fellowman, includes family members and non–family members, and it is true that sometimes we have to choose between loyalty to Jesus and loyalty to blood relatives (Matthew 10:34ff; Luke 14:26). God always comes first. And yet even if the Bible teaches that we are to put God before our families, we are still to put our families before all other persons.

One of the most challenging verses in the entire Bible, 1 Timothy 5:8, addresses those believers who presumptuously expect the church to take care of their aged relatives when it is in their power to help them: *"And whoever does not provide for relatives, and especially for family members, has denied the faith and is worse than an unbeliever"* (NRSV).

Of all the family relationships, the Bible has the most to say about the marriage relationship. In fact, there is far more about husbands and wives, including marriage principles, than there is about children or parenting advice. As Paul says:

> [28]In this same way [as Christ loved the church], husbands ought to love their wives as their own bodies. He who loves his wife loves himself. [29]After all, no one ever hated his own body, but he feeds and cares for it, just as Christ does the church—[30]for we are members of his body. [31]"For this reason a man will leave his father and mother and be united to his wife, and the two will become one flesh." [32]This is a profound mystery—but I am talking about Christ and the church. [33]However, each one of you also must love his wife as he loves himself, and the wife must respect her husband (Ephesians 5:28–33).

This famous marriage passage stretches from Ephesians 5:21 to 5:33. It is thirteen verses long, while the parenting passage that follows is only four verses long:

[1]Children, obey your parents in the Lord, for this is right. [2]"Honor your father and mother"—which is the first commandment with a promise—[3]"that it may go well with you and that you may enjoy long life on the earth."

[4]Fathers, do not exasperate your children; instead, bring them up in the training and instruction of the Lord (Ephesians 6:1–4).

Why is there so much more biblical material, especially in the New Testament, on marriage than there is on being a father or mother? We believe that's because the better the marriage, the better the parenting. Part of parenting, after all, is showing your kids how to love the one you promised to love and be faithful to "till death do us part."

Spouse comes before all other human relationships, and that includes children! All too frequently, once the babies begin to arrive, husband and wife grow distant from one another. But if the Bible makes anything clear, it's that the husband-wife relationship deeply affects the children. This relationship is prior to and—in a sense—more important than the parent-child relationship. When we favor a child over our spouse, we are undermining the very basis of security that the child needs in order to grow up with a sense of well-being, confidence, and trust. Worse, if we are not respectful towards our spouse, that disrespect will affect how our children relate to the opposite sex! Of course we are not saying that we should neglect the basic needs of a defenseless baby in order to see to our marital pleasures and whims. There are those who abuse their children; God will not countenance such sin, and his penalties will surely be severe. Having made these qualifications, spouse still comes before children, and the children need to know this.

A secular psychotherapist once visited a house-church meeting in our home. I was exceptionally encouraged to hear her response after I asked her opinion about the key to well-behaved children. She replied, "It's the marriage." I nearly said "Amen!" It was reassuring to hear biblical wisdom coming from a professional counselor. Of course, parents naturally take care of their children (2 Corinthians 12:14), so children immediately follow spouse in the divine order. We are to favor our own children over "church friends" and the lost, even though fellowship with other Christians is vital, and outreach to the unsaved is also essential. We would encourage you fathers to spend individual times with your children, every week if possible.

So far, based on the biblical evidence, we have arrived at the following relational priorities:

1. GOD
2. SPOUSE
3. CHILDREN

But what about everybody else—those not in your immediate family? We can distinguish between believers and nonbelievers, not because this is a convenient division, but because the Bible itself makes this very distinction. For example, consider Galatians 6:10:

[10]Therefore, as we have opportunity, let us do good to all people, especially to those who belong to the family of believers (NIV).

Other versions, instead of "the family of believers," read "the household of (the) faith" (HCSB, NASB); "the family of faith" (NRSV); "our Christian brothers and sisters" (NLT); or "the people closest to us in the community of faith" (The Message). The apostle Paul is referring to the church family. Who are your church family? They, *not* the lost, come next in the sequence. Paul made that clear. He is certainly not saying that we shouldn't try to be a light in the community, share the gospel with others, or push ourselves to be outgoing, even to the point of initiating conversations with strangers. What he is saying is that we are to honor our spiritual family—our brothers and sisters in Christ—above outsiders.

Nor is Paul saying that it is okay to ignore the lost in the name of church obligations, any more than it is legitimate to

ignore children for the sake of spouse. It is not a matter of culti-
vating the higher-priority relationships and ignoring the others;
all must be pursued simultaneously. But when push comes to
shove, when a decision must be made, the priorities are clear.

Please don't misunderstand. Evangelism is a command of
Christ that applies to all believers. And yet the New Testament
emphasizes relationships with fellow Christians—"one-another
relationships"—far more than reaching out to the lost. Could
it be that if we focused more on our one-another relationships
(exhorting one another, speaking the truth to one another,
serving one another...), evangelism would take care of itself?
We think so.

Once again, we are obligated to reach out to insiders and
outsiders alike. And yet there is a ranking: insiders first, then
outsiders. Also, in a number of passages the immediate family
takes precedence over others (e.g., 1 Timothy 5:8).

Another reason the church comes between family and
the lost is that the church family is ultimately an extension of
our own nuclear families, in all their dynamics and patterns of
interaction. A spiritual congregation with strong nuclear families will display a tight-knit fellowship. And that is bound to be
attractive to outsiders.

Putting it all together, the ladder of earthly relationships
looks like this:

1. GOD
2. SPOUSE
3. CHILDREN
4. THE CHURCH
5. THE LOST

Counterproductive Counseling

Remember this sequence; it is integral to good parenting.
Unfortunately, it is not usually respected, even though there are
loads of scriptures to back it up. For example, instead of focusing
(*up the ladder*) on God [1] when my marriage [2] is hurting, I am
tempted to pour my life into others (*down the ladder*) [3, 4, 5]. It

is usually easier to work a rung or two down the ladder than to focus on the real issues. But if anything, an improvement at a higher level will benefit relationships lower down. The human tendency to focus downward instead of respecting the divine order is counterproductive and leads to confused and unhelpful counseling when we are trying to advise others.

To illustrate further, our children may be acting out, and through various incentives or disincentives I may try to change their behavior [3], when the real problem is between me and my spouse [2]. Or church relationships [4] may be suffering from disunity, resentment, and gossip. And yet the preacher is mostly concerned with bringing in new members [5]—oblivious, it appears, to the dysfunctional quality of the fellowship the newly evangelized are joining. There are times, we believe, when we should "clean our own house" before inviting the neighbors over.

Let's consider one last scenario. A husband and wife have unresolved issues. Rather than facing them and being willing to talk them through to resolution, the husband decides that the solution is to find a new non-Christian to reach out to. He may even insist on bringing the newcomer home, even though his wife is dying inside and wishes they as a couple would just get help. Of course, the outsider is initially impressed with the husband—his enthusiasm and apparent concern—but his wife knows the truth. His evangelism is only increasing the tension! In the process, the kids, who wish they had more time with their father, also end up feeling second rate. The wife is now convinced that he is a hypocrite at heart. The truth is, it is easy for many men, and not a few women, to lose themselves in evangelism—with the tragic effect that they end up losing their families, too.

How do I (Douglas) know about these mistakes? From making all of them myself.

The human tendency is to look at the surface, not to go to the source (1 Samuel 16:7, etc.). If you are running a high fever, putting ice on your skin is not the ultimate solution. We must probe deeper to understand the cause of the fever. If steam and blue smoke are pouring out from under the hood of your car, the problem is not with the tires or the sun visor—it's somewhere under the hood. In the same way, God's word tells us where to look:

- If the marriage is struggling, look one level *up*. Take an honest look at your spouse's walk with God—and also at your own.
- If the kids are acting out, look *up*—at the marriage!
- If the church is not a happy place, look *up*—at the nuclear families it comprises.
- If the lost are not attracted to the community of faith, look a level *up*—how are relationships in the body of Christ?

Summary

We must recognize the basic truths that flow from the divine ordering of relationships:

- All other relationships depend, ultimately, on one's relationship with God.
- When children arrive on the scene, couples must make the conscious decision to prioritize their marriage relationship.
- Kids observe the spirituality of and interactions between Mom and Dad, and are profoundly shaped by them.
- The church family is merely an extension of the nuclear families of the church, especially the families of principal leaders.
- While our mission is to seek and save the lost (Luke 19:10), this must not be raised above the biblical imperative to excel in one-another relationships.

Conclusion

If we follow these priorities, our children will not resent us; they will rather covet the secret of our joy and spirituality. And, in the process, they will be given the greatest possible opportunity to make their decision to become disciples of Jesus Christ.

When you are counseling others (Romans 15:14) and deciding how to use your time relationally, keep this "ladder" in mind. It will help us better love our spouses, parent our children, and build a godly family.

In the following section, we'll turn our attention to parents. Usually (though not always) when kids are acting out, the roots of the problem lie in the parents' lives. Culture and past family sins may play into the equation. In the next chapter we will begin with a study of parental modeling. In Chapter 7, we will study the parents of three special children in Israelite history. Then, Chapters 8 to 10 will focus on mothers, fathers, and "the Proverbs 31 woman." (And the Proverbs 31 man, too!)

Parents

Model Parents

"The scribes and the Pharisees sit on Moses' seat; therefore, do whatever they teach you and follow it; but do not do as they do, for they do not practice what they teach" (Matthew 23:2–3 NRS).

Parenting and building a godly family require more than making the home a haven or simply understanding the divine ladder of relationship priorities. If children are to feel a connection to God and become godly themselves, they will need to see it modeled.

If you are like most parents, you probably don't view yourself as *model* parents. And yet that is what you are: functioning as a model to your child. "Monkey see, monkey do," as the old adage goes. (Those with younger children may be tempted to smile at the image conjured up by this saying!)

As noted before, although there are numerous parenting principles in God's word, there is still far more material in the Bible on marriage (and adult relationships) than on parenting (and childhood issues). Considering how important the parenting enterprise is, one wonders whether the lack of explicit "parenting material" in the Scriptures points to a more significant reality. Since children learn largely by observing, demonstrating the kind of people we should be may be the best tutorial we can ever give them. Didn't Jesus himself place a similar emphasis in the Sermon on the Mount? (Matthew 5–7). This collection of sayings focuses on what we *are*, more than on what we *do*. No lecture speaks as loudly as a consistent life lived in accordance with God's word. In short, we must model it!

Joash and Jehoiada: The Power of a Guardian
You may feel at a loss when it comes to modeling, especially if you are parenting alone. Perhaps you are a widow or
widower. You may be divorced or were never married. Maybe
you are separated from your spouse for the time being or are
an adoptive parent experiencing difficulties with your adopted
child. Perhaps your spouse is disinterested in the children or
expects you to do all the work. Or maybe you are a guardian,
like Jehoiada, the shining star in the story below. Whatever your
situation, the principles of the Bible apply to you—even if you're
not raising a child in the context of marriage.

Yes, the good news is that there is hope! You can do something to shape your child's character. Do not underestimate the
power of a godly life lived in view of a child. To illustrate, let's
turn our attention to the eighth-century-BC boy king Joash. He
lost his father, Ahaziah, when the zealous Jehu assassinated
him. While his siblings were being executed by Ahaziah's mother, who was greedy for power, his half-sister hid him until the
strategic time.

> [10]When Athaliah the mother of Ahaziah saw that her son
> was dead, she proceeded to destroy the whole royal family
> of the house of Judah. [11]But Jehosheba, the daughter of King
> Jehoram,…took Joash son of Ahaziah and stole him away from
> among the royal princes who were about to be murdered and
> put him and his nurse in a bedroom. Because Jehosheba, the
> daughter of King Jehoram and wife of the priest Jehoiada, was
> Ahaziah's sister, she hid the child from Athaliah so that she could
> not kill him. [12]He remained hidden with them at the temple of
> God for six years while Athaliah ruled the land (2 Chronicles
> 22:10–12).

Athaliah was the grandmother of Joash. She was a wicked woman but a strong leader, and she seized control of the
southern kingdom of Judah and ruled it for six years. Jehoiada,
the elderly guardian of Joash, knew that the ungodly Athaliah
was ruining the nation, and he had the nerve to depose her once
the time was right.

Joash was still in the nursery when Jehoiada "adopted" him, and lived to the age of forty-seven. Jehoiada lived to 130, and several years after his death Joash defected from the Lord. This suggests that Jehoiada was at least in his sixties or seventies when he took Joash under his wing. Here follows the account of one of the many coups d'état of the Bible. Please keep in mind that the child is Joash, and his guardian is Jehoiada.

> [1]In the seventh year Jehoiada showed his strength… [3]The whole assembly made a covenant with the king at the temple of God.
>
> Jehoiada said to them, "The king's son shall reign, as the LORD promised concerning the descendants of David…"
>
> [10]He stationed all the men, each with his weapon in his hand, round the king—near the altar and the temple, from the south side to the north side of the temple.
>
> [11]Jehoiada and his sons brought out the king's son and put the crown on him; they presented him with a copy of the covenant and proclaimed him king. They anointed him and shouted, "Long live the king!" (2 Chronicles 23:1, 3, 10–11).

After the evil Athaliah is removed from power, righteousness begins to flourish in Judah. A general "housecleaning" begins, and young Joash is officially enthroned.

> [16]Jehoiada then made a covenant that he, the people and the king would be the LORD's people. [17]All the people went to the temple of Baal and tore it down. They smashed the altars and idols and killed Mattan the priest of Baal in front of the altars.
>
> [18]Then Jehoiada placed the oversight of the temple of the LORD in the hands of the priests…to present the burnt offerings of the LORD as written in the Law of Moses, with rejoicing and singing, as David had ordered…[20]and brought the king down from the temple of the LORD. They went into the palace through the Upper Gate and seated the king on the royal throne. [21]All the people of the land rejoiced, and the city was calm, because Athaliah had been slain with the sword (2 Chronicles 23:16–17, 18–21).

Joash is now king. (Technically speaking, Jehoaida is regent, reigning in place of the child.) We continue the story:

> ¹Joash was seven years old when he became king, and he reigned in Jerusalem for forty years… ²Joash did what was right in the eyes of the LORD all the years of Jehoiada the priest…
>
> ⁴Some time later Joash decided to restore the temple of the LORD. ⁵He called together the priests and Levites and said to them, "Go to the towns of Judah and collect the money due annually from all Israel, to repair the temple of your God. Do it now." But the Levites did not act at once.
>
> ⁶Therefore the king summoned Jehoiada the chief priest and said to him, "Why haven't you required the Levites to bring in from Judah and Jerusalem the tax imposed by Moses the servant of the LORD and by the assembly of Israel for the tent of the covenant law?"…
>
> ¹³The men in charge of the work were diligent, and the repairs progressed under them. They rebuilt the temple of God according to its original design and reinforced it (2 Chronicles 24:1–2, 4–6, 13).

The boy king begins his forty-year reign well. After some time, he restores the lapsed temple and even challenges his guardian, Jehoiada, to expect more of the priests and Levites, So far, so good. (Very good, so it seems.)

> ¹⁴As long as Jehoiada lived, burnt offerings were presented continually in the temple of the LORD.
>
> ¹⁵Now Jehoiada was old and full of years, and he died at the age of a hundred and thirty. ¹⁶He was buried with the kings in the City of David, because of the good he had done in Israel for God and his temple.
>
> ¹⁷After the death of Jehoiada, the officials of Judah came and paid homage to the king, and he listened to them. ¹⁸They abandoned the temple of the LORD, the God of their fathers, and worshiped Asherah poles and idols. Because of their guilt, God's anger came upon Judah and Jerusalem. ¹⁹Although the LORD sent prophets to the people to bring them back to him, and though they testified against them, they would not listen.
>
> ²⁰Then the Spirit of God came upon Zechariah son of

Jehoiada the priest. He stood before the people and said, "This
is what God says:'Why do you disobey the LORD's commands?
You will not prosper. Because you have forsaken the LORD, he
has forsaken you.'"
   ²¹But they plotted against him, and by order of the king
they stoned him to death in the courtyard of the LORD's temple. ²²King Joash did not remember the kindness Zechariah's
father Jehoiada had shown him but killed his son, who said as
he lay dying, "May the LORD see this and call you to account" (2
Chronicles 24:14–22).

When Jehoiada dies, and his spiritual influence is no longer
shaping Joash, the boy king quickly declines. He becomes worldly and even murderous. He has Jehoiada's son Zechariah (not
the minor prophet by that name, but a different man) executed
for challenging his sin! As a result, the Lord does call him to
account, in accordance with the words of the dying Zechariah:

   ²³At the turn of the year, the army of Aram marched against
Joash… ²⁴Although the Aramean army had come with only a few
men, the LORD delivered into their hands a much larger army.
Because Judah had forsaken the LORD, the God of their fathers,
judgment was executed on Joash. ²⁵…They left Joash severely
wounded. His officials conspired against him for murdering the
son of Jehoiada the priest, and they killed him in his bed. So he
died and was buried in the City of David, but not in the tombs
of the kings (2 Chronicles 24:23–25).

Lessons Learned
What a tragic ending! Joash had been doing so well. What
does this story illustrate? What are the lessons we can glean
for our own parenting?

•   When children are young, they need a guardian—a parent or
    other adult role model—to both protect and influence them.
•   Joash grew in conviction and took a stand, under the influ-
    ence of a man of God. He was not sentimental regarding his
    grandmother, but followed the law of the Lord despite the
    inherent risks.

- Even though Jehoiada and his wife were not legally Joash's parents, they served in this capacity, protecting and bringing him up in the instruction of the Lord. God worked through the situation, even though not within the context of a standard nuclear family.

- Despite the historic tendency for the temple worship to become compromised and corrupt, Jehoiada was still supportive of God's plan, and his positive disposition seems to have rubbed off on Joash. In the same way, no Christian congregation is perfect; even the best has its share of problems. It would have been easy for Jehoiada to become disillusioned, and for apathy, disconnection, or cynicism to have turned the young Joash against "church things" altogether.

- Jehoiada's willingness to serve as a guardian for Joash led to a spiritual revival in Judah (even if short-lived). Don't sell yourself short. Kindness and spirituality will affect a child significantly, and through that child, many, many others.

- There is no favoritism with God. For all the good of his earlier years, Joash's apostasy nullified his good record. (The entire chapter of Ezekiel 18 speaks to this situation.)

- Despite the sustained positive spiritual influence of the guardian (Jehoiada), Joash as an adult forsook the Lord. This seems to be an exception to the general truth of Proverbs 22:6. (More on this in Chapter 13.)

Further Biblical Principles

Jehoiada is far from the only example of a guardian in the Bible. There is Mordecai, who brought up Esther and through her saved the Israelites from destruction (Esther 1–10). Or take the mentoring influence of Elijah on Elisha (1–2 Kings), or Paul's well-known and fatherly relationship with Timothy, whose father was not a Christian (Acts 16:1–5; 1 Corinthians 4:17; 1–2 Timothy). The list goes on...

We close the chapter with a few key principles related to parental modeling. Please think about them and ask how they come into play in your own role as a mother or father.

- Consistency is paramount, and children expect it in parents. A parent or guardian who claims to be following Christ but is not exhibiting the fruit of the Spirit is an impediment to a child's decision for Christ. Kids grow resentful when they sense hypocrisy or double standards (for further study, see Romans 2:1–3; Matthew 7:1–5; Matthew 23, especially verse 13; Mark 7:6–8; Luke 6:40–42; Galatians 2:13; James 3:17; 1 Peter 2:1).

- Modeling does not work *only* by behavior. Words are important, too. Ephesians 6:4 reads, *"And now a word to you fathers. Don't make your children angry by the way you treat them. Rather, bring them up with the discipline and instruction approved by the Lord"* (NLT). We are to actively talk about God's word with our children (Deuteronomy 6:7). Words alone are not enough, but then neither are actions alone sufficient.

- According to Proverbs 22:6, the training we give to our progeny tends to stay with them. While this verse is only a generalization, it is still a valid observation of the usual linkage between godly instruction and future faithfulness. (For further discussion on whether this verse is meant to be interpreted absolutely and without exceptions, see Chapter 13).

- In terms of guidance, try to strike a balance. While discipline is important, if we are too hard on the children, they will lose heart. *"Fathers, do not embitter your children, or they will become discouraged,"* we read in Colossians 3:21. The NASB reads, *"Do not exasperate your children"*; the NKJV, *"Do not provoke"* them.

- We need to model respect if we expect our children to be respectful to us and others. So many adults in our society speak and act disrespectfully towards others: family members, the government, seniors, children, those from other cultures, etc. We live in an increasingly disrespectful world, and if we will only model respect, our children will shine like stars in contrast to all the darkness and negativity around them.

- Your spiritual influence—for good or for bad—is significant. Don't think that only the influences of outsiders will affect your children. We are all affected in one way or another by those we spend time with (1 Corinthians 15:33), and nowhere is this truer than in the case of one's own family members.

- And yet the influence of parents does not work mechanically or fatalistically. Ezekiel 18:14, 17 NRSV reads, *"If this [wicked] man has a son who sees all the sins that his father has done, considers, and does not do likewise...he shall surely live."* Modeling provides a general prediction of how the children will turn out. It does not absolutely guarantee anything. "The acorn does not fall far from the tree," they say, and "Like father, like son." It is certain that all children become like their parents, at least in some ways. But every individual is different and makes individual choices. Your children are not *destined* to become one particular sort of person, based on genetics, church situation, culture, or even your own spirituality, despite the correlations. Through the power of the Holy Spirit, we can beat the odds.

- Be careful about dealing with your own issues (church issues, especially) in front of the children. *"Do not let any unwholesome talk come out of your mouths, but only what is helpful for building others up according to their needs, that it may benefit those who listen"* (Ephesians 4:29). If this is true of our speech in the presence of other adults, how much more does it apply to our children! They are affected by our spirituality (or lack of it), and pick up on the words and tone we use to talk about "church stuff." The kids may be more perceptive than we think! So if we must talk about sensitive matters, let's be discreet, remembering the warning of the Lord in Luke 17:1–3a: *"Things that cause people to sin are bound to come, but woe to that person through whom they come. It would be better for him to be thrown into the sea with a millstone tied around his neck than for him to cause one of these little ones to sin. So watch yourselves."*

- Let's consider one last principle, from 2 Timothy 2:23–26:

> [23]Don't have anything to do with foolish and stupid arguments, because you know they produce quarrels. [24]And the Lord's servant must not quarrel; instead, he must be kind to everyone, able to teach, not resentful. [25]Those who oppose him he must gently instruct, in the hope that God will grant them repentance leading them to a knowledge of the truth, [26]and that they will come to their senses and escape from the trap of the devil, who has taken them captive to do his will.

When we instruct our children, we must watch ourselves lest we become impatient or resentful (if the children are resisting our input). It is ultimately up to God to move in the hearts of our children, both during the few years we have them in our care, and afterwards.

Conclusion

Certainly we do not want to be like the religious leaders Jesus excoriated in Matthew 23, who did not practice what they preached. Through godly words and godly actions, we have the opportunity of a lifetime to influence the young "Joashes" the Lord has put in our care. Let's model what we believe, and let's practice what we preach. For whether or not we feel like model parents, we are most certainly parental models.

In the next chapter we will study the little-known, but fascinating, Nazirite parents.

Be the Parent!

"I also raised up prophets from among your sons and Nazirites from among your young men. Is this not true, people of Israel?" declares the LORD (Amos 2:11).

Families and other social units are not only increasingly dysfunctional, but also characterized by inversion. Children tell their parents to shut up. Worse, the parents obey!

I remember well an incident in my first grade class. I was all of six years when I bluntly told our teacher, Mrs. Belden, "Shut up." She marched me to the sink, and in full view of all twenty-something students, washed out my mouth with soap. I needed that! Never again did I mouth off to a teacher. (Not to say I was never the class clown.) Yet these days, a teacher who took a firm charge of her or his students would be fired, and perhaps even imprisoned. How far we have fallen!

Consider how many inversions now mark our society:

- Children rule the roost, with parents expected to be passive witnesses.

- Students are often arrogant, disruptive, and even abusive towards their teachers—and too many parents take their children's word over the teacher's.

- Penalties for crimes against animals (especially when they are protected species) are often stiffer than crimes against humans.

- Government "servants" enrich themselves, reinforcing power structures and social inequalities, instead of leading by example. Yet Jesus taught, *"You know that those who are regarded as rulers of the Gentiles lord it over them, and their high officials exercise authority over them. Not so with you. Instead, whoever wants to become great among you must be your servant, and whoever wants to be first must be slave of all"* (Mark 10:42b–44).

- Virtue is mocked, while vice is lauded—and even constitutionally protected. *"Woe to those who call evil good and good evil, who put darkness for light and light for darkness"* (Isaiah 5:20).

- Outward appearance trumps inner qualities in a global beauty market that has topped $275 billion, the opposite of Peter's teaching in 1 Peter 3:3–4.

- Homosexuality is considered the most natural thing in the world, contrary to Romans 1:26–27. Some even say that gender has no biological basis but is an entirely social construct.

- The lost don't need saving. Rather, the saved need to be "saved" from their delusion that anyone might be lost!

These inversions are powerful currents coursing through the warp and woof of society, and it takes a lot of courage to resist them.

This chapter identifies the good that accrues when we actively parent, and the bad when we are passive, caught up in role inversions. Our angle of approach will be to consider three parenting case studies.

Now, Who Are the Nazirites?

Nazirites—most folks have never heard of them! In fact, when we ran a spell check on this chapter, the dictionary thought we had made a spelling error. It suggested that we had meant to type "Nazi rites"! (Now let us assure you that that is absolutely the last thing we would want to commend to you in a parenting book, no matter what you may think about some of our firmer conclusions.)

Three Special Children

Amos, writing in the eighth century BC, reminded the Israelites of the special leaders God had given to them (2:11). The Nazirites were special children, and their parents must have had high hopes for them. According to Numbers 6:1–8, the classic Nazirite text, they were to follow several additional commandments not required for other Jews:

> [1]Then the LORD said to Moses, "Speak to the people of Israel and give them these instructions: [2]If some of the people, either men or women, take the special vow of a Nazirite, setting themselves apart to the LORD in a special way, [3]they must give up wine and other alcoholic drinks. They must not use vinegar made from wine, they must not drink other fermented drinks or fresh grape juice, and they must not eat grapes or raisins. [4]As long as they are bound by their Nazirite vow, they are not allowed to eat or drink anything that comes from a grapevine, not even the grape seeds or skins.
>
> [5]"They must never cut their hair throughout the time of their vow, for they are holy and set apart to the LORD. That is why they must let their hair grow long.
>
> [6]"And they may not go near a dead body during the entire period of their vow to the LORD, [7]even if their own father, mother, brother, or sister has died. They must not defile the hair on their head, because it is the symbol of their separation to God. [8]This applies as long as they are set apart to the LORD."

The vow contains three stipulations: abstinence from alcohol, not cutting one's hair, and avoiding dead bodies. The Nazirite vow was not necessarily lifelong, as 6:13–22 goes on to explain, although Samson's vow did apply to his entire life.

This lesson is *not* about the three most famous Nazirites of the Bible, Samson, Samuel, and John—even though they are far more illustrious than their fathers and mothers—but about their parents! There is something in here for all of us; everyone falls somewhere along the spectrum.

Three Sets of Parents

Samson's parents were too soft on their only child (Judges 13:3–5, 8–14, 24–25, 16:17–19). They failed to instill discipline, character, and spirituality. In their case, we find weak parents trying to manage a strong-willed child. They are older—not itself a disqualification—but they are also out of touch.

Samuel's parents, Hannah and Elkanah, exhibit a deeper level of involvement with their son (1 Samuel 1:10–2:1). They were concerned that their child be brought up in the faith, but were unfortunately not involved enough to ensure that he would be able to bring up his children in the fear of the Lord.

Finally, Zechariah and Elizabeth, parents of John the Baptist, exerted a strong godly influence on him (Luke 1:5–7, 23–25, 39–45, 57–66). Their son displayed self-control, humility (John 3:30), and deep conviction (Malachi 3:1–2, 4:6; Luke 3). Their parenting was excellent. We see improvement as we move through time (from the twelfth century BC to the eleventh to the first) from each set of parents to the next, though none are perfect. And now let us examine the three families one by one.

Manoah and Wife

Manoah and his wife have no children when we meet them in Judges 13. The setting is more than three thousand years ago, in the chaotic period of Israelite history between the conquest of Canaan and the monarchy.

> [1]Again the Israelites did evil in the eyes of the LORD, so the LORD delivered them into the hands of the Philistines for forty years.
>
> [2]A certain man of Zorah, named Manoah, from the clan of the Danites, had a wife who was sterile and remained childless. [3]The angel of the LORD appeared to her and said, "You are sterile and childless, but you are going to conceive and have a son. [4]Now see to it that you drink no wine or other fermented drink and that you do not eat anything unclean, [5]because you will conceive and give birth to a son. No razor may be used on his head, because the boy is to be a Nazirite, set apart to God from birth, and he will begin the deliverance of Israel from the hands of the Philistines."

⁸Then Manoah prayed to the LORD: "O Lord, I beg you, let the man of God you sent to us come again to teach us how to bring up the boy who is to be born."

⁹God heard Manoah, and the angel of God came again to the woman while she was out in the field; but her husband Manoah was not with her. ¹⁰The woman hurried to tell her husband, "He's here! The man who appeared to me the other day!"

¹¹Manoah got up and followed his wife. When he came to the man, he said, "Are you the one who talked to my wife?"

"I am," he said.

¹²So Manoah asked him, "When your words are fulfilled, what is to be the rule for the boy's life and work?"

¹³The angel of the LORD answered, "Your wife must do all that I have told her. ¹⁴She must not eat anything that comes from the grapevine, nor drink any wine or other fermented drink nor eat anything unclean. She must do everything I have commanded her."

¹⁷Then Manoah inquired of the angel of the LORD, "What is your name, so that we may honor you when your word comes true?"

¹⁸He replied, "Why do you ask my name? It is beyond understanding." ¹⁹Then Manoah took a young goat, together with the grain offering, and sacrificed it on a rock to the LORD. And the LORD did an amazing thing while Manoah and his wife watched: ²⁰As the flame blazed up from the altar towards heaven, the angel of the LORD ascended in the flame. Seeing this, Manoah and his wife fell with their faces to the ground. ²¹When the angel of the LORD did not show himself again to Manoah and his wife, Manoah realized that it was the angel of the LORD.

²²"We are doomed to die!" he said to his wife. "We have seen God!"

²³But his wife answered, "If the LORD had meant to kill us, he would not have accepted a burnt offering and grain offering from our hands, nor shown us all these things or now told us this" (Judges 13:1–5, 8–14, 17–23).

Samson is to be a Nazirite. Not all Israelite boys and girls were expected to enter into such a vow, which represented a higher calling. God always had special purposes in mind for those under the Nazirite vow.

Notice his father's reluctance to believe all of his wife's initial report after encountering the angel. He accepts the broad outline, but feels he must hear for himself the rules for bringing up this special child. As a result, the angel has to repeat the instructions already given. (This is not an uncommon theme in the Scriptures: men's unwillingness to trust the messages relayed by women!—Luke 24:9–11; Acts 12:12–15, etc.) Note also her common sense, in contrast to his emotional reaction on realizing they were speaking to an angel—"We are doomed to die!" Had his father been more levelheaded, one can only think that Samson would have benefited. At any rate, the angel's words came true.

> [24]The woman gave birth to a boy and named him Samson. He grew and the LORD blessed him, [25]and the Spirit of the LORD began to stir him while he was in Mahaneh Dan, between Zorah and Eshtaol (Judges 13:24–25).

At last Samson is born, and the Spirit of God moves him in a special way. God had intended all along to use Samson, through the unique gifts conferred on him, to hasten the liberation of Israel from their Philistine overlords.

> [1]Samson went down to Timnah and saw there a young Philistine woman. [2]When he returned, he said to his father and mother, "I have seen a Philistine woman in Timnah; now get her for me as my wife."
> [3]His father and mother replied, "Isn't there an acceptable woman among your relatives or among all our people? Must you go to the uncircumcised Philistines to get a wife?" (Judges 14:1–3).

Here we see the impulsive, sensual, unspiritual side of Samson. He may be the strongman of the Bible, but his strength was carnal, not spiritual. He was led by his eyes, and as a result not only married outside the faith (against God's revealed will in both testaments—Exodus 34:16, Deuteronomy 7:3; 1 Corinthians 7:39; 2 Corinthians 6:14, etc.), but also compromised the security of Israel. His parents had given up trying to deter him. They apparently knew that once Samson has made up his mind, it was not worth the struggle trying to make him change it. What heartache Manoah and his wife must have suffered with such a headstrong child!

It is a reasonable inference that the pattern of manipulation and ineffective parental response goes back to Samson's childhood. Evidence for this possibility is found in Judges 14:10ff, where Samson, who was a clever youth, tells a riddle in order to extort gifts from his groomsmen. When we consider how Samson's mind worked, we begin to appreciate not only his intelligence but also his dexterity at getting what he wanted. Such behavior is consistent with the manipulative child, always trying to "reason" with his parents. (We know all about this. Our first strong-willed child broke us in, and by the time our second came along, we were more or less prepared. Child number three had a different personality type, and the lesson applied less to her.)

Incidentally, when Samson killed the young lion and again returned to its carcass (Judges 14:6–9), he violated his Nazirite vow. The verse in Numbers 6 is clear: *"And they may not go near a dead body during the entire period of their vow to the Lord."* Samson more than once got as close to sin as he could—and then crossed the line. Such was his lack of self-control. In addition, his presence at the wedding party (14:10, 17)—considering that the story of his life reads like that of a juvenile delinquent—suggests that he was not careful to avoid alcoholic beverages, either.

We know the familiar story of this "judge" of Israel, which spans four chapters in the book of Judges. When at last Delilah coaxes the secret of his phenomenal strength out of him, he tells her about his Nazirite vow. (Not that all Nazirites had superhuman strength; the connection seems to be fortuitous.) So he tells her everything. *"No razor has ever been used on my head,"* he said, *"because I have been a Nazirite set apart to God since birth. If my head were shaved, my strength would leave me, and I would become as weak as any other man"* (Judges 16:17).

To sum up, Samson's parents were weak, and he manipulated them. They failed to instill depth of character and spirituality.

They are typical of naïve, "old-fashioned" parents who don't understand the modern world. They do not seem to have taught their child to say no to sin. A modern-day Samson might have charged down the path of substance abuse: alcoholism, ecstasy-fueled "raves," or hard drugs. Samson would undoubtedly have excelled at sports and been popular with the girls. If this is your child, watch out! You may have a Samson in your house. Without the limits needed to keep him on the straight and narrow, Samson would roam anywhere he wanted. His parents would never "ground" him, take his driver's license away, or fail to give him the money he needed to finance his sin binges. Are we in touch with what the world is throwing our children's way? And are we in touch with our children's feelings? Or are we out of touch, unaware, and underappreciating the forces that threaten to mold them in ungodly ways?

Yes, Samson *did* make a grand comeback at the end of his life (Judges 16:28–30), but only after the consequences of many impetuous decisions had ruined it. We like to think that shorn, blind, and pensive, he at last learned from his heavenly Father the spiritual lessons his earthly father had failed to teach him. After all, he is ranked among the great men of faith in Hebrews 11:32, so let's not be too hard on him. Besides, our focus in this study is not on the child, but on the parents.

Hannah and Elkanah

We are still in the period of the Judges when we meet Hannah and Elkanah, the mother and father of Samuel, though now at the end of this painful period in Old Testament history. God, through Samuel, would institute the monarchy. Though the first king was a failure, his successor, David, was a glorious success. Not that he was perfect, but still, he is celebrated in both testaments as "a man after God's own heart" (2 Chronicles 16:9; Acts 13:22).

Like Samson's parents, Elkanah and Hannah had had no children, at least not together. Elkanah's other wife had borne him several children (1 Samuel 1:2, 4), and this made Hannah's "infertility" all the more vexing.

[10]In bitterness of soul Hannah wept much and prayed to the LORD. [11]And she made a vow, saying, "O LORD Almighty, if you will only look upon your servant's misery and remember me, and not forget your servant but give her a son, then I will give him to the LORD for all the days of his life, and no razor will ever be used on his head."

[12]As she kept on praying to the LORD, Eli observed her mouth. [13]Hannah was praying in her heart, and her lips were moving but her voice was not heard. Eli thought she was drunk [14]and said to her, "How long will you keep on getting drunk? Get rid of your wine."

[15]"Not so, my lord," Hannah replied, "I am a woman who is deeply troubled. I have not been drinking wine or beer; I was pouring out my soul to the LORD. [16]Do not take your servant for a wicked woman; I have been praying here out of my great anguish and grief."

[17]Eli answered, "Go in peace, and may the God of Israel grant you what you have asked of him."

[18]She said, "May your servant find favor in your eyes." Then she went her way and ate something, and her face was no longer downcast.

[19]Early the next morning they arose and worshiped before the LORD and then went back to their home at Ramah. Elkanah lay with Hannah his wife, and the LORD remembered her. [20]So in the course of time Hannah conceived and gave birth to a son. She named him Samuel, saying, "Because I asked the LORD for him" (1 Samuel 1:10–21).

Hannah had vowed that if God did give her a child, she would literally give him over to the Lord, presenting him to the leadership at Shiloh, the site of the tabernacle at that time. The Lord opens her womb—another recurrent biblical theme—and in the course of time Samuel is born. (For more on the common situation of the wife unable to have children, see Genesis 20:17–18, 29:31, 30:22; Deuteronomy 28:4; etc. Besides the mothers of Samson, Samuel, and John the Baptist, another well-known woman in the same category is Rachel.)

Hannah is a model of faith and prayer, and there are numerous intentional parallels between the present account, involving her and Samuel, and the account of Mary and Jesus in Luke 2. (Mary, another woman of prayer, even addressed God in language harking back to Hannah's exact phraseology in 1 Samuel 2.)

> [21]When the man Elkanah went up with all his family to offer the annual sacrifice to the LORD and to fulfill his vow, [22]Hannah did not go. She said to her husband, "After the boy is weaned, I will take him and present him before the LORD, and he will live there always."
>
> [23]"Do what seems best to you," Elkanah her husband told her. "Stay here until you have weaned him; only may the LORD make good his word." So the woman stayed at home and nursed her son until she had weaned him (1 Samuel 1:21–23).

Notice Elkanah's interaction with his wife. He respects her judgment (the decision not to "go to church"). A man's respect for his wife is the key to a healthy marriage and healthy parenting. Moreover, his chief concern is that the vow to the Lord be fulfilled. Elkanah is definitely *not* Manoah! On the other hand, he leaves it to his wife to bring the boy to the tabernacle.

The obvious question for fathers is, do you leave it to your wife to see to the spiritual needs of the children? Fathers need to be involved. Elkanah seems to have been a good man, but he could have been a better one had he been more involved in his son's spiritual development.

> [24]After he was weaned, she took the boy with her, young as he was, along with a three-year-old bull, an ephah of flour and a skin of wine, and brought him to the house of the LORD at Shiloh. [25]When they had slaughtered the bull, they brought the boy to Eli, [26]and she said to him, "As surely as you live, my lord, I am the woman who stood here beside you praying to the LORD. [27]I prayed for this child, and the LORD has granted me what I asked of him. [28]So now I give him to the LORD. For his whole life he will be given over to the LORD." And he worshiped the LORD there (1 Samuel 1:24–28).

Eli is the chief priest in Israel, and true to her word, Hannah gives her son over to his care. Samuel also lives from this time, if not earlier, as a Nazirite. Interestingly, one of the Dead Sea Scrolls (4QSama) refers to Samuel as "a Nazirite forever all the days of his life." Hannah stays connected to her son, visiting him (at least) annually, but for all intents and purposes he is in the care of the "children's ministry."

Eli becomes the surrogate father, a sort of "single parent" bringing up the boy Samuel, who in due time will eclipse him as Israel's true spiritual leader. Eli is no paragon of spirituality, and his abysmal parenting of his ungodly sons, Hophni and Phinehas (not to be confused with the righteous Phinehas of Numbers 25 fame), ranks among the worst in the Bible. We do not have time to explore 1 Samuel 2, but if you are unfamiliar with this woeful account, we encourage you to read it before proceeding.

The point is that even though spirituality around "the church" (the tabernacle) was suboptimal, to put it mildly, Samuel still turned out well. He was godly, affected many others for good, and was used greatly as the pivotal figure between the judges (of whom he was the last) and the kings (the first of whom he appointed in 1 Samuel 9). And he, like Samson, appears in "the hall of fame of faith," in Hebrews 11:32.

As an after-note, Samuel himself was not well equipped to bring up his own children in the way of the Lord. His "foster father," Eli, had turned a blind eye to the sin in his own family. Presumably his weak example of parenting affected Samuel, whose sons did not walk with the Lord as their father did.

Church leaders *do* influence our children. Both they and their families will be closely watched, and the good and the bad cannot be covered up. Perhaps because Samuel, from a young age, was not brought up in a functioning nuclear family, he did not know how to father his children with the wisdom and spirituality that characterized other areas of his life.

When all is said, Samuel's parents were much more successful than Samson's. That's because they were more spiritual. Their primary concern was that their son be brought up in the faith. Is this your primary concern (as opposed to education, comfort, athletics, popularity, health, or looks)?

Zechariah and Elizabeth

Our final couple, like the first one, was advanced in years and had not been able to conceive a child. The following scene takes place more than a millennium after the previous one:

> [5]In the time of Herod king of Judea there was a priest named Zechariah, who belonged to the priestly division of Abijah; his wife Elizabeth was also a descendant of Aaron. [6]Both of them were upright in the sight of God, observing all the Lord's commandments and regulations blamelessly. [7]But they had no children, because Elizabeth was barren; and they were both well on in years (Luke 1:5–7).

During one of Zechariah's terms of service at the temple in Jerusalem, the angel appears to him and announces some good news—even though he is a bit reluctant to believe it and is punished for his lack of faith by being struck dumb for the greater part of a year! This consequence—a discipline from God—may have served to teach Zechariah a valuable lesson. Then as now, when the family knows that the head of the family is on track spiritually (receiving input and correction as needed), it is easier for them to submit to God themselves.

> [23]When his time of service was completed, he returned home. [24]After this his wife Elizabeth became pregnant and for five months remained in seclusion. [25]"The Lord has done this for me," she said. "In these days he has shown his favor and taken away my disgrace among the people" (Luke 1:23–25).

Elizabeth, the now pregnant wife of Zechariah, is Mary's blood relative—which will soon make her son, John, a cousin of Mary's son, Jesus.

> [39]At that time Mary got ready and hurried to a town in the hill country of Judea, [40]where she entered Zechariah's home and greeted Elizabeth. [41]When Elizabeth heard Mary's greeting, the baby leaped in her womb, and Elizabeth was filled with the Holy Spirit. [42]In a loud voice she exclaimed: "Blessed are you among women, and blessed is the child you will bear! [43]But why am I

so favored, that the mother of my Lord should come to me? ⁴⁴As soon as the sound of your greeting reached my ears, the baby in my womb leaped for joy. ⁴⁵Blessed is she who has believed that what the Lord has said to her will be accomplished!" (Luke 1:39–45).

Their reunion is filled with emotion. Each of them will give birth to a child who will change the world—although of course on vastly different scales! It may also be significant that Elizabeth sought moral support from another believer (Mary) as she was bringing her child into the world. Relationships with dear friends who can relate to our local home or church situations can be sources of mutual encouragement and strengthening. This, of course, indirectly benefits our children.

⁵⁷When it was time for Elizabeth to have her baby, she gave birth to a son. ⁵⁸Her neighbors and relatives heard that the Lord has shown her great mercy, and they shared her joy.

⁵⁹On the eighth day they came to circumcise the child, and they were going to name him after his father Zechariah, ⁶⁰but his mother spoke up and said, "No! He is to be called John."

⁶¹They said to her, "There is no one among your relatives who has that name."

⁶²Then they made signs to his father, to find out what he would like to name the child. ⁶³He asked for a writing tablet, and to everyone's astonishment he wrote, "His name is John." ⁶⁴Immediately his mouth was opened and his tongue was loosed, and he began to speak, praising God. ⁶⁵The neighbors were all filled with awe, and throughout the hill country of Judea people were talking about all these things. ⁶⁶Everyone who heard this wondered about it, asking, "What then is this child going to be?" For the Lord's hand was with him (Luke 1:57–66).

At this time the newborn is to receive his name. Culture and family tradition dictate that the child be named after his father. (How does "Zach the Baptist" sound?) And yet the Lord had previously revealed that the son was to be named John. Rather than capitulate to family and social pressure, Zechariah and Elizabeth do what is right. Against considerable pressure, they stand their ground and are unwilling to compromise. Such firmness in parents is a spiritual quality, and obviously affected their special child.

And so John the Baptist enters the world. What kind of a person is he? Self-controlled. Frugal. And godly. He calls people back to the law of God, just as the prophecy in Malachi 4 had foretold. Moreover, he is humble. As he said of Jesus, *"He must become greater; I must become less"* (John 3:30). That's a good prayer for all of us to say: "Jesus must become greater; I must become less."

John prepared the way for the Lord. By the time his ministry was underway, it is quite possible his aged parents had already died. Was he the perfect child? Or the perfect man? No. Even John had his period of doubt (Luke 7:18–23). But once again, the spotlight is not being shined on John here. It's on his parents. They were godly, deeply involved in "church," and their Nazirite son—most Old Testament scholars consider him to have lived as a Nazirite (see Luke 1:15, 7:33)—was extraordinarily strong spiritually.

Similarities and Differences

All three couples were faithful within their marriages, although it appears that the wives were more spiritual, or at least more prayerful, than their husbands. Two of the three couples were aged, and all by the time we meet them would otherwise have been well down the road to building families. All strongly *wanted* children. (The challenge for us is to continue to "want" our children when the going gets tough.)

All three couples depended on the Lord for the birth of their special child. (We know that many of our readers can relate!) All three had a son who was dedicated to the Lord in a unique (Nazirite) way and became an influential leader in Israel. All three sons were gutsy. Two were imprisoned at the time of their death, and all three were faithful to God when they died. Samson and Samuel are both listed in Hebrews 11, and John the Baptist may also be included there generically (*"still others were chained and put in prison"*—Hebrews 11:36).

Yet Samson's parents were weak; they were not sufficiently

involved in the character development of their son. Although Manoah should have been more sobered than he was through the encounter with the angel, he does not seem to have changed appreciably as a result. This in contrast to Zechariah, who took a stand after his sobering (and humbling) angelic encounter. (Men, are you quick to change when you receive spiritual input?) In Samson's family, it appears the boy was leading his parents, not the other way around. In our families, we should be willing to ask the honest question, who is leading whom? Samuel's parents were better, although entrusting him to the soft, indulgent Eli probably diminished Samuel's overall impact on Israel. His father seems to have been less involved than he could have been, leaving it to his mother to look after Samuel, and then to the "foster father," Eli. Still, Samuel was not a worldly man, and judged Israel with integrity.

John's parents were the most successful of the three, and brought up a child who stood boldly for the cause of the Lord. He feared God far more than he feared men. Nor was their son worldly. Much of John's spiritual strength and resolve can be attributed to the faithful spirit of Zechariah and Elizabeth, two godly individuals we meet at the opening of Luke's gospel.

Conclusion

The three sets of parents brought up their children with varying degrees of success. On the scale of weak to strong parenting, where do you fall?

If we want our children to be devoted to the Lord and set apart for a godly life, this will require a high degree of involvement from us. We will need to keep the pledges and resolutions we have made about our sons and daughters. Words alone are not enough. Instruction in the word of God is necessary, and parental modeling also makes a tremendous difference in the spiritual growth of a child. Parental involvement and firmness, however, are indispensable.

Words, actions, involvement—this is not passive parenting. We must *be the parents.* Our biological contribution to our child's genetic makeup most emphatically does not qualify us as parents. Parenting must be intentional and along the lines God has laid out in his word.

Mothers: Balancing It All

You must teach what is in accord with sound doctrine… teach the older women to be reverent in the way they live, not to be slanderers or addicted to much wine, but to teach what is good. Then they can train the younger women to love their husbands and children, to be self-controlled and pure, to be busy at home, to be kind, and to be subject to their husbands, so that no one will malign the word of God (Titus 2:1–5).

Up Against a Wall!

I (Vicki) had the babysitters all lined up and their instructions written out. The dinners were prepared and in the fridge, the lunch boxes were ready, and breakfast was finished. Even the suitcase was packed (I could read my Bible on the plane). Now all I had to do was get three kids off to three different schools, and then drive to the airport. Easy!

But suddenly, after a smart-aleck comment from my son, James, I "lost it" that September morning. I spun out. I hit the proverbial wall. I sinned and was out of control, and wanted to physically hurt my child. I had my nine-year-old up against the wall by the neck, and was verbally threatening him. (Sure, he'd been disrespectful, but where had my reaction—all that rage—come from?)

I'll never forget the sheer fear on his face, the tears in his eyes, the shock and surprise as I went out of control. I had done what I thought I would never do. I shouted, yelled, was physically threatening, and wanted to knock some sense into him, out of sheer frustration.

Was this really me? What *were* my convictions, after all?

Weren't my roots supposed to be in God's word? Certainly I was under a lot of pressure, but that day I was 100% in the wrong. James bore the brunt of my anger and my sin. I was so ashamed, but I also knew that deep down I was a shallow parent. I had gone against all the principles I believed in, and I needed help from the word of God. It felt as if I were the one up against a wall!

Time to Reconsider

This incident helped me to realize how self-reliant I had become. I was on "autopilot" and without a plan or direction for how to be a spiritual mother. I had coped for years and had been "strong," but what were my convictions based on? Remembering the Parable of the Soils, I felt spiritually as though I were being choked out by the thorns (Luke 8:14).

Mothers have amazing resilience and coping mechanisms, but we all hit the wall and fail at some point if we don't have deep roots and a strong relationship with God. For us mothers, circumstances keep changing, and we need firm convictions about motherhood if we are to keep our balance. At first, when you have a child, it all seems so natural. Children are added to the family, and the family develops quickly. But just as a tall tree requires deep roots and a skyscraper is only stable when built upon a deep foundation, so our families need deep roots in the principles of God's word.

If the foundation of our home isn't deep enough, it is unsteady. My foundation was shaken. Like the foolish woman of Proverbs 14:1, I felt like I was tearing down my own house. I needed help, and I needed to be honest. You know deep inside when you're unraveling spiritually. I needed to confess my sin to God, to my husband, and also to a wise friend. And I needed to apologize to my child. I had to repent, to make a decision to prioritize my relationship with God, and to search the Scriptures so that I would have biblical convictions—not just convenient notions about how to spin all the plates. It was time to be honest and sort out the real issues and differences between my husband and me (marriage issues that affected our parenting and home life) and come up with a plan about how to put into practice the principles in God's word.

Once I started to study in earnest, many passages started to make sense. As I share about the scriptures I reexamined after the incident with my son, I would like to begin with my study of Mary, the mother of Jesus.

A Mother Who Balanced It All

Who is your role model for motherhood? Your own mother? A Christian sister whom you admire and respect? Or maybe you look to a woman in the Bible. (If so, who is it? Martha, worried and upset? Or Sarah, Hannah, Moses' mother, the Proverbs 31 woman, or Elizabeth?) My heroine and model is Mary, the mother of Jesus.

Mary was chosen by God to bear his child (Luke 1–2). As a person, she was cool, calm, and collected. She was content with her role (Luke 1:38) and allowed her husband, Joseph, to take the lead. Submitting to our husbands is not so difficult if we have submitted ourselves to God first (1 Peter 3:1–5). Mary trusted not only God, but also her husband. Joseph was a godly man and protected his wife. He was willing to marry her even though she was pregnant and he was not the father. Young mothers need protection, both emotionally and physically.

We too should be calm. Part of the secret is anticipating that there will be emergencies, even ones that involve our children. Accidents happen. How we respond depends on our faith in God. If we are like Mary, we will not be rattled, but will trust the Lord and *respond* appropriately. If we are not prepared, then when hard things happen, we will *react*. We too can remain cool, calm, and collected, if we imitate the faith of Mary.

Mary was flexible and unflappable, despite pressures that would have been overwhelming for most parents (Matthew 2:13–22). Even when worrisome and puzzling words were spoken to her (Luke 2), she was not reactionary. Instead, she pondered the words and grew in wisdom and understanding. With such a well-balanced and godly mother, it is no wonder Jesus was such an amazing child! Yours too is amazing. (How well do you know your child?)

Mary was also a joyful person (Luke 1:46–47). The atmosphere in the home is largely determined by you as a mother. In your home, is there a dark cloud hanging over everyone's head, or is your house filled with laughter and joy? When you instruct your children, are your words patient and positive, or irritated and threatening?

When Jesus was twelve years old (Luke 2:42), Mary was disappointed, and seems to have taken it personally, that Jesus stayed back in Jerusalem (Luke 2:48). Yet at that time she was only in her twenties. By the time we see her in her mid-forties, she is becoming more controlling (Mark 3:21, 31; John 2:3–5). She was probably in menopause at that time, and perhaps like many of us during that stage she was becoming a little fearful about life. When we are fearful, we tend to try to control, even if that means "taking" control from God to ensure that bad things do not happen. It is hard for us, when we are fearful or insecure, to let go. Joseph apparently was not alive, and to make things worse, her eldest son (she had five, according to Matthew 13:55), was a little "out there."

Mary does seem to be in control of her emotions at the cross (John 19:25–27). Perhaps a few years of Jesus' ministry were finally getting through to her, and she was accepting the inevitable: his death. At any rate, by Acts 1:14 she has joined the apostles in their prayer meeting.

I see Mary as wise, understanding, and someone who had the "big picture" of what was happening. She was not always as understanding, but she worked through her doubts and came to a point of faith and trust. She evidently recalled and thought through all the great things and prophetic words said about Jesus, and she became his follower.

Although all four of her other sons were among the believers at the start of Acts, her sons James and Jude became especially influential in the early church, and both of them wrote letters in the New Testament.

Training in Titus 2

After my disturbing "wall" incident with my son, another passage I reread was Titus 2, and I realized it applied to me. I needed to be *trained* how to love my husband and children, just as the Scriptures said.

> ³Teach the older women…to teach what is good. ⁴Then they can train the younger women to love their husbands and children, ⁵to be self-controlled and pure, to be busy at home, to be kind, and to be subject to their husbands (Titus 2:3–5).

Loving newborns is easy. But as the children grow up, they are not always as loveable as when they were cute, helpless babies. In the same way, it is easy to love our husbands when we are newlyweds. But as the years go by, things change and we can take each other for granted. It's at that time that we need help from outsiders. Keep in mind these principles:

- *Training:* Mothers and wives need help from older women, who have much to share because of their years and experience.

- *Protection:* Love always protects (1 Corinthians 13:7). It doesn't harm (Romans 13:10).

- *Communication:* I realized that if I was upset with Douglas, I could easily take it out on James, who from time to time reminded me of his father's weaker points. I needed to "work *up* the ladder" of priorities (see Chapter 5), and not focus on James. Douglas and I needed to work on our communication and marriage. My husband and I were so very busy, but not "busy at home." In our marriage we had a strong commitment (one aspect of love), but we had lost a lot of the friendship of earlier years. Things were "functional." We had a divide-and-conquer mentality when it came to getting things done, but we were isolated from one another. Can you relate?

The Wife of Noble Character

Another passage I turned to was Proverbs 31:10–31. I re-envisioned the "wife of noble character," and realized that she worked—but from her home. As a church worker for many years, I had the businesswoman as my mental model, and in terms of working with my husband, we had viewed our ministry as a fifty/fifty proposition. We both worked, so we should divide our domestic duties equally—so we reasoned. But this did not work well in practice, and our family lacked cohesiveness.

We recognized the reality that the family really needed *both* of us. Neither of us had had good limits up till this time, and we had to start setting some if we were to protect our family. We also came to accept that I could not be the mother I felt God was calling me to be while keeping up the same pace as Douglas.

Eve as a Helper

Genesis 2, another significant passage for me, talks about the wife being the husband's helper. Some women object that it is degrading to women to call her man's helper. But this is the same Hebrew word used of God himself! (Genesis 49:25; Psalm 30:10, etc.). It is not degrading, but a high calling.

For Douglas to be a father *and* do his job, I needed to be a support and a helper. And we needed to be on the same page. I came to the conviction to travel less. In biblical times, husbands would leave their families and go to Jerusalem, and the wives didn't always follow. I didn't have to go to everything—how freeing that insight was!

Then we talked about the kind of mother Douglas wanted me to be. That meant, however, that *he* needed to change, to support and protect me so that I would have the "space" required to be a mother. Fortunately, he was more than willing. It was going to take two of us to change the direction of our family.

I also thought about how bad it would be to stand before God at the last day having neglected an orphan. We had had the privilege of adopting Lily, but was I only providing a roof over her head and giving her a "better life," a higher standard of living, or was I providing a home, a haven, a family? *"God sets the lonely in families"* (Psalm 68:6). Lily had been neglected once. She needed security, as did our other children. And with God's strength, as a mother I was in the position to provide exactly that.

It took a few months to get everything in place and everything turned around, but soon I was really enjoying being a mother again. Douglas and I could now see the value God had placed on motherhood, and also the respect that Jesus had for mothers in the New Testament. I accepted God's plan and embraced it. I was going to be content in my role, especially for the next ten years until the children were launched.

Serving the Lord

I came to see that I must be willing to deny myself and not cling to "my time," certainly as long as the children still lived at home. Letting go helps me appreciate God's plan and find my security in him alone. Colossians 3:23 says we should do whatever we do wholeheartedly, since we are actually serving the Lord. Yes, the cooking and cleaning and ironing can be a chore, but I am grateful now for the time I had to be at home and bring up the children.

During that period, I no longer worked outside the house. I think we made less money than we had even ten years prior, and for several years we had to go without any vacation. We didn't eat out so much anymore, nor did we have as many clothes as we used to. But we were a happy, fulfilled, fun-loving family, looking forward to the days to come and definitely enjoying the teen years. And the fun hasn't stopped!

I hope that the scriptures I have shared about—the passages that helped me as I rethought motherhood—will prove helpful to you, too.

Balancing It All with Two Careers

Maybe you are a "working mother," one who has a job outside the home. But as we know, *all* mothers work. And they work hard! Adding a *second* job or career will stretch you to your limits. Before we go any further, some words of qualification are in order. We fully realize that in some family situations, mothers have no choice but to work away from the home.

We have nothing but respect for those brave souls who are working two jobs (one outside the home and one in it)! Please understand that the following discussion is based on what has been generally observed in society. It is also based on biblical principles. Every situation is different, and parents must make their own decisions about how to apply the principles.

We all have seen the stats on percentages of working women in the United States. When Douglas and I were growing up, the overwhelming majority of married women carried on the noble work of homemaking and childrearing, while their husbands provided for the family financially. Women did not feel too much pressure to "make something of themselves"—even those with college degrees. Both of us grew up in families where our mothers stopped working (outside the home) while the children were still at home. We appreciate that they did this for us.

And yet things changed through the turbulent '60s and '70s—the Sexual Revolution, the Feminist Movement, and the antiestablishment, antiauthoritarian streak left our world forever changed. Despite the positive contributions of the Feminist Movement, it was largely responsible for the change. No longer was being a homemaker a worthy ambition. "Not working" was a stigma, and motherhood came to be viewed as a lesser calling than a professional vocation.

Today the vast majority of wives work outside the home; children are regularly farmed out to daycare centers and other providers. Many feel more fulfilled having careers as doctors, lawyers, and business executives. Mothers in two-income families may claim they cannot "survive" with only one income. Perhaps more significant, they are under pressure from their husbands to work. This is not just a matter of keeping up with the Joneses; servicing debt (mortgages, various loans, and above all, monthly credit card payments) has created a bondage which cripples family life and leaves couples with no choice but to bring in two incomes.

Is the extra income really necessary? The typical American home in the '00s is more than double the floor space of the typical home in the '50s or '60s. The fact is, much of the increase from dual incomes is eaten up in higher taxes, daycare costs, and other expenses incurred as a result of the fatigue the working mother suffers trying to cope with day-to-day life.

Despite all these negative effects, most of us have bought right into this thinking. Sadly, American society at large, though never technically Christian, has departed significantly from biblical mores. The dual-income model has both catalyzed this change and been accelerated by it. What are the fruits of our society's more "enlightened" approach to the institutions of work and family?

- Unhealthy pressure levels have psychosomatic effects. Many women are in poor health.

- Kids are relegated and delegated to secondary caregivers, and may become resentful. They can also become worldly, affected by non-Christian attitudes.

- "Quantity time" (essential to effective parenting) degenerates to "quality time" (the tacit admission that other things are more important).

- Women feel persistent, nagging guilt for not taking care of those they love most (husband and children).

- Marital problems are rampant.

- Depression, medication, and therapy are commonplace. Dysfunction manifests itself in so many ways!

Many women are working more hours outside the home than necessary. We need to have more empathy and recognize that women are created differently from men—in constitution and in emotional makeup, to speak generally. But society has pushed women to prove their "worth." Even in Christian circles, women may seek approval through immersing themselves in church programs, to the detriment of their home life. In part, this is because appreciation is too seldom expressed for all that mothers do—especially by their own families.

Interestingly, in Titus 2:1–5, Paul classifies his instructions regarding domestic things as a matter of "sound doctrine." There are quite specific instructions for older men, older women, and younger women. (The passage goes on to cover the younger men and slaves.) The Greek word for sound also means healthy. Healthy doctrine enables us to be healthy spiritually, and the Bible's teaching about family life is an important part of sound doctrine. The Bible puts a high premium on home life, while the world often makes women (and men) feel second class who choose to devote themselves to their children instead of to careers.

A few years back, in the magazine *Washingtonian* there appeared an article in which it was posited that having children was a sure way to slow down one's career and detract from self-fulfillment. It was proposed that we should forego having children if we really want the most out of life. Kids are, it was implied, a total nuisance. We were not the only ones disturbed by the article and finding it in bad taste, and my husband decided to phone one of the editors and have a chat. She told him that many had been upset by the feature, which had actually been intended "as a provocative joke." Yet if this was so obviously a joke, why did so many persons take it seriously? Surely because it strikes so close to home. It is common in our culture to sacrifice family for career achievement to the point that family disintegrates. This is a far cry from the original plan of God for happy marriages, spiritual children, and striving together for common goals as a family.

The attitude that children get in the way of career is reflected in the corporate world. A survey of well-paid academics and businesswomen revealed that 42% of them were still childless at age 40 to 55. Fortunately, the pendulum is beginning to swing the other way. Also, it is becoming easier to work from one's home, thanks to home offices and computers with high connection speeds. But regardless of which way our culture drifts, we need to look to the word of God for our guidance.

Conclusion

Motherhood is a high calling, even though our society fails to value it as it should. Not all mothers can stay at home with their children, but those who can and do should be respected, not disrespected. And if they are able to work from their homes, maximizing time with the kids, then they are getting the best of both worlds.

Let's all make sure our roots are deep in the word of God. Then, when tough times come—as they will!—we will be ready for them, stable and not easily toppled.

In the next chapter we move from motherhood to fatherhood.

Fathers: "Forceful Men"

And, Fathers, do not provoke your children to anger; but bring them up in the discipline and instruction of the Lord (Ephesians 6:4 NASB).

Note: This is a chapter for fathers, though mothers are welcome to listen in! I (Douglas) am a father of three. I have not always lived by the principles I advocate in this chapter, though I'm trying to lead my family differently. In the meantime, until I "arrive" (at the last day, of course!), faithfulness to the gospel requires that I teach these principles to others, even if I'm applying them to my own situation only imperfectly.

Fatherhood is a position of both responsibility and leadership. As Christian fathers, we are likely to lead with certain preconceived ideas: our own father's leadership style; the demeanor of a respected authority in our lives; the drive of various sports heroes or business executives; and (quite likely) the disposition of church leaders in our local congregation. That is why it is important at this time to take something of a detour. Everything on this tangential itinerary applies, directly or indirectly, to fatherhood—so please stay tuned.

Forceful Men

Church leadership seminars stress the need for "forceful men" (and women) in positions of spiritual leadership. We study the lives of great athletes and CEOs as we search for inspiring examples of leadership in the world to rouse churches out of lethargy. The more powerful the leader, the more hope we feel. "Certainly the principles of leadership are the same, whether inside or outside the church," we think.

Yes, it is true that Christian churches need men and women of conviction and drive to step up and lead. Yet does the Bible teach that one of the primary qualifications for a man of God is to be "forceful"? Where do the Scriptures tell us to be "forceful"— which easily approximates "determined to get our way"?

In Matthew 11, Jesus upholds a *gentle* style of leadership. This passage also contains excellent parenting principles, since Jesus was the Master Teacher and molder of character:

> [28]"Come to me, all you who are weary and burdened, and I will give you rest. [29]Take my yoke upon you and learn from me, for I am gentle and humble in heart, and you will find rest for your souls. [30]For my yoke is easy and my burden is light" (Matthew 11:28–30).

In spite of this, the original NIV translators managed to make a passage sixteen verses earlier teach the exact opposite— or at least that's the way many see it.

> [12]From the days of John the Baptist until now, the kingdom of heaven has been forcefully advancing, and *forceful men* lay hold of it (Matthew 11:12 NIV 1973–1984, mistranslated).

But is this what the word of God really says? Why do other versions render the Greek very differently?

> [12]From the days of John the Baptist until now, the kingdom of heaven has been suffering violence, and *the violent* have been seizing it by force (HCSB).

> [12]And from the days of John the Baptist until now the kingdom of heaven suffers violence, and *the violent* take it by force (KJV).

> From the days of John the Baptizer until now, the kingdom of heaven has suffered violence, and *violent people* are taking it by force (from the Greek, my translation).

As you will probably have guessed from the words I emphasized in the verses above, the wording "forceful men" is found only in the NIV. I have checked another fifteen English versions, as well as another fifteen languages, yet not one agrees with this unusual rendering, which appeared from 1973 to 1984 and was corrected when the TNIV New Testament came out in 2002:

> ¹²From the days of John the Baptist until now, the kingdom of heaven has been subjected to violence, and *violent people* have been raiding it (Matthew 11:12 TNIV, NIV 2011).

The Original Greek

In Matthew 11:12, the "forceful men," in the original Greek, *biastai*, are literally violent persons, not men of noble character. They are revolutionaries, zealots, and brutal men. In the Bible, they are rioters, persecutors, terrorists, and slave drivers. These are not the sorts of people you want to serve under, or whom you want to be making decisions that affect the lives of your friends and family. And you, as father to your children, most certainly do not want to emulate them. This single mistranslation—unfortunately in the most popular Bible version of our day—has made many un-Christlike fathers and leaders (insecure, angry, or pushy) feel justified.

The NIV mistranslation has lamentably led to wrong theology. Not a few people have been hurt because of the misunderstanding of Matthew 11:12.

Let's also turn to the Old Testament for an example of a leader who tried to be "forceful" (actually driven to this by his own insecurity and emotional immaturity). Our man is Rehoboam, the son and successor of Solomon, around 930 BC. He consulted his contemporaries, other young men not yet seasoned by life and all too eager to advise a hardline approach to royal leadership:

> ⁹[Rehoboam] asked them, "What is your advice? How should we answer these people who say to me, `Lighten the yoke your father put on us'?"

> [10]The young men who had grown up with him replied, "Tell these people who have said to you, `Your father put a heavy yoke on us, but make our yoke lighter'—tell them, `My little finger is thicker than my father's waist. [11]My father laid on you a heavy yoke; I will make it even heavier. My father scourged you with whips; I will scourge you with scorpions'" (1 Kings 12:9–11).

Unfortunately, although the elders gave the correct counsel (1 Kings 12:6–8), Rehoboam, in a show of bravado, repeated the very words of his young (and errant) advisers. The result was that the kingdom of Israel split in two. People simply didn't want to be under his harsh leadership.

Anger

Let us consider another example of "forceful" leadership. (In fact, just about every leadership lesson there is applies to fatherhood in one way or another.) Moses *forcefully* expresses his anger towards the people of God after he comes down from Horeb (Numbers 20). He *violently* smashes the tablets and forces the people to drink the water into which the tablets have been pulverized. This action, though extreme, is neither commended nor condemned in the Exodus record.

Yet in Numbers 20 we see that Moses, in unbridled *anger*, uttered harsh words and struck the rock instead of speaking to it as God had commanded. In so doing, Moses dishonored God. Even though he achieved his short-term objective—water flowed from the rock—he had disobeyed God. As a result, he was not permitted to enter the promised land. With this in mind, one consequence of the mistranslation of Matthew 11:12 is that when men lose their temper they feel justified. Another is that, like Moses, those who don't control their tempers miss out on some of God's blessings.

Such anger and forcefulness can spill over into the pulpit—preachers angrily confronting congregations even when it is not called for. Another obvious arena is the home. How many "forceful" leaders have wounded their wives and children through outbursts of anger? I have known far too many husbands—including Christian leaders—whose wives, sons, and daughters have become the targets of their temper. This tends to crush their spirits and sap their joy (Ephesians 6:4). We know that love is not easily angered or provoked (1 Corinthians 13:5). Wrath is something we had best leave to the Lord. Unrighteous anger has evil consequences. Forceful anger is nearly always hurtful, if not destructive. In fact, anger may be the number one sin for most fathers, and I am not unfamiliar with this sin personally.

Although not a person who expresses anger or frustration by "erupting," venting, or even shouting, I am aware that in my heart there can be anger and negativity. Since I tend to hold it in, to internalize my emotions, when it does find expression it easily hurts others. This can take the form of sarcasm, belittling comments, or just an "edge" to my words. I am also aware that when I have unresolved issues, it affects my public speaking. I may be unnecessarily strong, or perhaps disengaged and not sufficiently connected with the audience. Anger, if not dealt with biblically, has to go somewhere, and it tends to hurt others when it is released.

Do you think something similar may be happening in your own life? Without the help of Vicki and the Lord, I would probably never make any progress in this area. I am trying to be a different husband, father, and man. Though I have far to go, I am working on it.

Righteous Anger?

Yes, it is true that Ephesians 4:26, quoting Psalm 4:4, instructs us, *"In your anger do not sin."* Not all anger is sinful, and it is possible to have righteous anger. In John 2, where Jesus in fiery zeal cleansed the temple, his passion was not for his own agenda, but for the Father's honor. Some angry church leaders claim to be representing the cause of God, whereas in fact they are irritated because members are not "on board." It is also true that some leaders in the Bible are charged to *"encourage and rebuke with all authority"* (Titus 2:15). But "authority" is not a synonym for "anger." Otherwise the verse could be read, "Encourage and rebuke with all anger."

This is clearly not what Paul is saying; how could anyone

encourage with all anger?

Another well-known passage is Matthew 23, where Jesus delivers a face-to-face challenge to the Pharisees for their hypocrisy and its influence on others. He called them "sons of hell" (v.15)—and he was in a position to know if this was the case. Strong words—but not too strong, considering the situation. Yet when a brother or sister is annoying, or has failed to support a leader's programs, such words are not only inappropriate, but also completely contrary to the spirit of Christ. The Lord is gentle, and he urges us to be the same (Ephesians 4:2).

So how can we distinguish appropriate anger? Paul was forceful in the "majors" of guarding doctrines that preserve freedom, and also in protecting the flock from the wolves. Yet he showed grace and flexibility in the "minors." Let the example of the great apostle, who was as close to the heart of Jesus as anyone, be our guide. (Even better, let Jesus be our guide!) Lack of conviction and passion is no virtue in a leader; and yet anger is a vice.

Input

In the decision-making arena, "forceful" husbands do not value input, tending to view themselves as experts and others as subordinates whose opinions are not particularly valuable. They may consider themselves to be "called by God." After all, why take input if you are somebody who claims, "The Lord has put something on my heart"? To challenge such a leader—would this not then be to call into question God himself?

God's Judgment?

In Jesus' lifestyle, speech, and manner of dealing with people, he demonstrated unmistakably that we are to be gentle, respectful, and kind. "Forceful" leadership is anything but that. To my shame, I admit that too often I have justified heavy-handedness in my life (and in others' lives) by Matthew 11:12. But as I have explained, I was wrong to apply the passage in this way. I am sorry. Further, "holding up our leaders' arms" (Exodus 17:12) never means condoning unrighteous anger, pushiness, or disrespect. That's because anger is usually a negative personality trait, not a positive one, and certainly not a virtue. I do not want to be known as an angry man. Do you? The Bible is replete with scriptures, especially in the Proverbs, urging us to seek input and not to think we have advanced to a point where it is no longer necessary (Proverbs 28:26, for example). There are also many accounts of men who would not listen, and ruined their lives and their families as a result. Saul, Nabal, and Shimei come to mind (all mentioned in 1 and 2 Samuel, and Shimei's end is recounted in 1 Kings).

The principle applies to church leaders as well as to parents. We all need input. And the more responsibility we have, the more we need it! (James 3:1).

Conclusion

Matthew 11:12 in the NIV was unfortunately mistranslated for almost thirty years. Among the English versions of the Bible, it apparently stands alone in its mistranslation, and has given justification to bullying behavior on the part of many fathers and Christian leaders. Theology is important; it generates and reinforces behaviors, whether godly or otherwise.

Let all talk of "forceful men" stop. There is no excuse for bullying. As fathers, we need to embody the strength of conviction *and* the gentleness of Jesus Christ. Gentleness is one of the fruits of the Spirit (Galatians 5:23). Are we gentle— physically, verbally, and emotionally? To the extent that we are not, we are falling short of the ideal of Jesus' character.

How do you know if you are an "angry father"? Is your wife "shut down," feeling unable to give you input or correct you on anything? Do you ever raise your voice at your wife or kids? Are your children buoyant and happy, or crushed in their spirit ("exasperated," as the Scriptures put it)? Are your kids expressive and giving, or quiet, secretive, eager to be away from home? (Are they even sneaking away?) Do your children feel comfortable coming to you and telling you when they feel you are "out of line," being too hard on them? Do not be deceived. If we as fathers are not spending quality *and* quantity time with our children, talking to them about real issues and listening to them, they will seek out others to talk to. Many children become sexually active in the teen years, in part because of their parents' (fathers' especially) emotional distance. We must strive for emotional connection with our kids.

Have you embraced a domineering, "take-charge," "type A" leadership style? Or are you striving to adopt the infinitely gentler approach of Jesus? Sure, there are times for anger, even in parenting. But they should be rare. Keeping anger godly is one of the most Herculean feats a human can achieve. Jesus exhibited anger only when God was being dishonored, or the helpless were being taken advantage of. There is no question that his indignation was righteous and thoroughly grounded in the word of God. Besides, we should remember that, even if wrath is an attribute of the Lord God, in Scripture he is consistently described as "slow to anger." See Exodus 34:6; Numbers 14:18; Nehemiah 9:17; Psalm 86:15, 103:8, 145:8; Joel 2:13; Jonah 4:2; and Nahum 1:3—all of these passages come from the Old Testament, not the New. Stern fathers, do you think God has become sterner in the New Testament?

As James wrote, *"My dear brothers, take note of this: Everyone should be quick to listen, slow to speak and slow to become angry"* (James 1:19). The words of James, if they are put into practice, describe a truly godly man. In a sense, the only "force" that should be present in a father is the force of the Holy Spirit, transforming his character and spiritually encouraging and energizing his family.

Fathers, do you feel the conviction of the Holy Spirit? Then let me urge you to study the following passages: Proverbs 15:1, 25:15; Zechariah 9:9; 1 Corinthians 4:21; 2 Corinthians 10:1; Ephesians 4:2; Philippians 4:5; Colossians 3:12; 1 Thessalonians 2:7; 1 Timothy 3:3, 6:11; 1 Peter 3:15. May the *gentle* force of the Holy Spirit course through our very veins.

And now, to "The Proverbs 31 Couple," and a chapter for both men and women.

The Proverbs 31 Family

A wife of noble character who can find?
She is worth far more than rubies (Proverbs 31:10).

"The Wife of Noble Character" is the crowning jewel in the collection of wisdom in God's word, the Wisdom Literature that includes not only the book of Proverbs, but also Job, Ecclesiastes, and the Song of Songs. Most lessons on this godly woman are just that—lessons on the woman. In this chapter we want to read between the lines and go behind the scenes. We are interested in the wife of noble character, but equally interested in the husband of noble character who evidently stands beside her.

The Woman

This woman is amazing. She is hardly the stereotypical, submissive, silent, servile, repressed woman of traditional society. That she exists at all should serve as a warning to us not to overgeneralize about the world, ancient or modern. She is so virtuous, one even wonders if she could be a real woman at all, as opposed to a composite of many exemplary mothers in ancient Israel!

This "ideal wife" leads a fulfilling life, even without a career outside the home. And yet her life does not exclude doing business. She is somewhere between the "traditional mother" and the "working mother." Careerism is in many ways the natural worldly response to the Feminist Movement, but the

Proverbs 31 poem is the perfect antidote to excessive emphasis on career. What strikes us in the famous eulogy of the wife of noble character?

- She takes care of her children. (Childcare is not exclusively delegated to others.)
- She is hardworking and industrious.
- She enjoys a measure of financial independence, and her husband trusts her with the checkbook.
- She conducts a business from within the home.
- Her home is exemplary and brings her husband honor in the public arena.
- Just as her husband provides for her, so she provides for him, and brings him credit.
- She and her husband complement one another. There is a healthy interdependence between the two of them.
- She is able to pass on what she has learned to others, through "faithful instruction" (see Titus 2:4–5).

In short, she excels in "domestic" qualities. Well, what else do we see?

- She has distinguished herself in bringing up faithful children.
- She has been excellent in the area of hospitality.
- She has "helped those who are in trouble"—a qualification involving the heart (mercy) and the head (practical assistance).

She has devoted herself to a variety of good deeds, though none is specified, but at this time we will explore her virtues no further. In the next section we will turn our attention to her counterpart.

A similar passage is 1 Timothy 5, a much neglected chapter. Here Paul lays out the requirements for being placed on the list of widows—that is, those older women who will receive support from the church. The widow needs to have lived a productive life, and this qualification is apparently expected to continue once she receives financial assistance from the congregation. This shows us that God values domestic qualities.

The Man

Who is the husband referred to occasionally in this poem? To piece together a picture of the husband and friend, we will need to (literally) read between the lines and consider the flip-side—what we will call the Proverbs 31 man. When Douglas and I teach marriage and parenting seminars, this is one of our favorite lessons.

Let's read through the passage again, with an eye on the man beside the woman:

> [10]A wife of noble character who can find?
> She is worth far more than rubies.
> [11]Her husband has full confidence in her
> and lacks nothing of value.
> [12]She brings him good, not harm,
> all the days of her life.
> [13]She selects wool and flax
> and works with eager hands.
> [14]She is like the merchant ships,
> bringing her food from afar.
> [15]She gets up while it is still dark;
> she provides food for her family
> and portions for her servant girls.
> [16]She considers a field and buys it;
> out of her earnings she plants a vineyard.
> [17]She sets about her work vigorously;
> her arms are strong for her tasks.
> [18]She sees that her trading is profitable,
> and her lamp does not go out at night.
> [19]In her hand she holds the distaff
> and grasps the spindle with her fingers.
> [20]She opens her arms to the poor
> and extends her hands to the needy.

²¹When it snows, she has no fear for her household;
 for all of them are clothed in scarlet.
²²She makes coverings for her bed;
 she is clothed in fine linen and purple.
²³Her husband is respected at the city gate,
 where he takes his seat among the elders of the land.
²⁴She makes linen garments and sells them,
 and supplies the merchants with sashes.
²⁵She is clothed with strength and dignity;
 she can laugh at the days to come.
²⁶She speaks with wisdom,
 and faithful instruction is on her tongue.
²⁷She watches over the affairs of her household
 and does not eat the bread of idleness.
²⁸Her children arise and call her blessed;
 her husband also, and he praises her:
²⁹"Many women do noble things,
 but you surpass them all."
³⁰Charm is deceptive, and beauty is fleeting;
 but a woman who fears the LORD is to be praised.
³¹Give her the reward she has earned,
 and let her works bring her praise at the city gate.

What did you notice?

- He has full confidence in his wife. Do you trust your wife? Does she feel that?

- He trusts her with domestic responsibilities. Men, do you?

- Notice her confidence. It may well be that he has been able to help her not to fear. Many women, as they grow older, become fearful in ways they were not when they were younger. But the Proverbs 31 woman has a bearing of confidence that speaks volumes of the sense of security her husband has brought into the home.

- He is gainfully employed and highly respected outside the house. This surely makes her life more of a joy and provides the context of security that facilitates family.

- He is able to serve as an elder (verse 23), and his wife and children are a credit to him. (If you are looking for an Old

Testament passage on an "elder's wife," here it is!)

- He allows her to have a modicum of financial independence. Most men seem to expect their wives to overspend. As a couple, they have not reached financial maturity in the marriage, and may be in competition for the checkbook. We must not be foolish, but expect the best of each other and work towards practical solutions to financial problems, each spouse taking part.

- He does not "control" her, but allows her to live her own life. She is not his personal servant, though she is a servant. Similarly, he is not detached or aloof; there is an emotional connection between them.

- He is positive about his wife and says affirming things about her. (And presumably not just on anniversaries and birthdays!)

- His children perceive their mother in a highly positive light. Certainly this is affected by their father's disposition. A man who disrespects his wife, silently or vocally and in earshot of the children, is weakening the fabric of his own family.

- He is not focused on the outward (her appearance and charm), but on character (her fear of God). This man has not bought into the lies of the world about beauty, femininity, and sexuality.

- Bottom line, he *respects* his wife. Women want to be loved and respected. In such an emotional climate, they will blossom.

The Family

Men, if you want a Proverbs 31 wife, you had better become a Proverbs 31 husband. Together you will be a rare and effective couple. Your children will be happy, emotionally healthy, and godly. In that sense, the "Proverbs 31 family" epitomizes God's ideal human family.

In the next section, "Children," we will probe character forma-tion, respect as the foundation for parenting, discipline (including positive and negative reinforcements), conversion, and adoption.

IV

Children

Character, not Personality

We also rejoice in our sufferings, because we know that suffering produces perseverance; perseverance, character; and character, hope. And hope does not disappoint us… (Romans 5:3–5a).

Character and Personality

Character is not the same thing as personality. Sometimes we say, "He's a real character!" But in this instance we're probably referring to someone's lively personality, or maybe even his eccentricities. But the Bible teaches us that character is *built by perseverance through difficulties over time* (Romans 5:3–5).

Whereas our basic personality type is fixed early on in life, character can grow. Personality is like the body type we were born with. Your skeletal frame is pretty much decided by genetics along with dietary habits in your early years. Character, on the other hand, is like muscle. Everyone has some, but in different degrees. Like muscle, character—with work—can be built. Likewise, with insufficient attention given, it can shrink. We can continue to mature in character as long as we breathe, not just during the formative years of early childhood. That is good news!

Genuine character is marked by such qualities as responsibility, unselfishness, honesty, integrity, and generosity. Such strengths are modeled by parents and, with good parenting, can even be transmitted from generation to generation, provided the children imitate the heart and behavior of their elders. (Of course, character flaws can also be transmitted generationally, as the Bible amply illustrates.) All of us want our children to grow up to be men and women of character.

The Outside vs. the Inside

The world looks at personality, the outside, but God searches for character, for "those whose hearts are fully committed to him," for the "man after [his] own heart" (2 Chronicles 16:9; Acts 13:22). It is relatively easy to play a role, to "act" like someone who has it all together. But it takes time to develop character. It will be worth the wait. Character, at the end of the day, is all that counts.

Our world is obsessed with glamour, and Hollywood makes actors into anomalies, with scads of money and scandals galore, but a deficit of character and seemingly little functional family life. Why are people so drawn to the gossip, the affairs, the big houses, and the predictable divorce? Isn't it all make-believe, "fairy tale" drama—and unhealthy at that? Some may not be allured by the world of actors and actresses, but they are infatuated with athletes, many of whom exhibit no more character or self-control than their counterparts in Hollywood. It is sad to meet so many children whose aspirations are to become NBA players or to go to the Olympics. It's not that these are necessarily bad things, but only an infinitesimal percentage of the population has what it takes to succeed along that route. These kids are setting themselves up for disappointment. For most of us, there simply is no quick way to make money, just as there is no shortcut to character development.

Something to Shoot For

In addition to time, developing character takes courage and patience. Obviously, deep down in our hearts we want to be like Jesus, and that is a lifelong, lofty, and worthy goal. Since we won't be arriving anytime soon, sometimes we can relate to other biblical figures, those whose situations we identify with and whose lives speak to us.

With this in mind, we try to imitate the godly attributes of men and women of faith in the Bible. Their lives provide a snapshot of what to shoot for. Think about some of the righteous lives lived by Old Testament individuals. We are aware, of course, that the Bible usually shows us the faults of its major figures, not just the glory. Yet righteousness shines through the pages of Scripture all the same. When we study out the persons in Hebrews 11, this becomes clear.

Of course, the ultimate role model for us all is Jesus Christ, who was not only overflowing with personality but also strong in character. Jesus was breathtakingly balanced in all areas of his life, so much so that no one area of strength stands out beyond another. He was, in other words, perfectly well rounded (Mark 7:37).

Daniel

We frequently see similarities between the strengths and even the weaknesses of people in the Bible and those of our own children. That gives us a picture, something to aim for, and a lot of hope. For our son, James, we see great value in studying out the character of the prophet Daniel. James is a bright young man, organized and determined. Daniel was wise, not just intelligent, using his gifts to bring glory to God when he was far from home. He took a stand and showed great insight. He was righteous and had good friends who were also contending for the faith and were not people pleasers. They were honest and open to God's truth. Daniel is the kind of role model we envision for James—not some notorious film personality from among the ranks of the "rich and shameless."

Rebekah, Rachel, et al.

For girls, like our daughter Emma, I (Vicki) put together a class series on "Teen Girls of the Bible." Young women we looked at included Rebekah, Rachel, Miriam, Mary, Esther, and even two servant girls (Rhoda and Naaman's servant). One of the points that emerged from the series was that these girls had pleasing dispositions. They were confident and could talk comfortably with men, and yet they were amiable and gracious. Today we see teen girls full of "attitude," and with few godly qualities. The honorable girls of the Scriptures were both trusting of their parents and eager to please God. Their parents had faith in them, not fear lest they turn away from the Lord. What great role models we can see if we search the Scriptures and teach from them! When we study the Bible, the text speaks for itself and produces lively discussion. For example, when we were reading about Rebekah's brother checking out her prospective suitor, we asked the girls a question: "How would you feel if your dad or brother chose your prom date?" Keep it real!

Esther

Lily, our youngest, has always loved the story of Esther. Nothing brings more comfort to her than this young orphan's courage. In fact, there are quite a few inspiring stories of adopted children in the Bible. How the Lord looked after them through caring souls allows us to see God's heart and character, lets us know we belong to him, and produces confidence, trust, and faith. One girl can change the course of history.

Conclusion

Character is not the same as personality. Everyone has personality, but not everyone has Christlike character. What are the lessons we learn as we study this biblical theme?

- It is the parents' God-given responsibility to help their children become people of character. It's *their* primary charge, not that of the schools, the youth ministry, or any other human agency.

- Biblical individuals provide far better role models than the rich and famous of the world, who many times are only role-*playing* anyway. After all, who do you want your child to grow up and be like? Joe Cool? Jane Glamour?

- It takes time to build character. As we saw in Romans 5, there is no easy way to build and enhance it. Character comes *by* perseverance *through* hardship *over* time.

Parenting is all about building character. This takes place through training and discipline, the subject of our next chapter.

Training and Discipline

Train children in the right way,
and when old, they will not stray (Proverbs 22:6 NRSV).

If we are going to "train [our] children in the right way" so that "when old, they will not stray," we need to build on the right foundation. The authority is the Scriptures, the Holy Bible. In addition, our relational priorities must be straight. As we discussed in Chapter 5, immediately after God comes spouse, not children. Children are third, ahead of just about everyone else in the world *except* for your husband or wife. If you want your parenting to go well, the best advice we can give you is this: Be content in your marriage. (And if you're a single parent, don't rush into marriage. You aren't at such a big disadvantage as you may think. It was not unusual in biblical times for a mother to have to bring up her children without the help of a husband.)

Expectations

Consistency of expectations leads to the goal, which is to have confident children. Inconsistency—announcing "rules" without following through on them—breeds not only contempt, but also insecurity. Kids want and need to know where "the line" is. Consistency is an expectation we should lay on ourselves. But what about expectations for the children?

To begin with, as someone said, "Kids will be kids." Let them enjoy life. Childhood is too short to squash it with an overbearing manner or legalistic micromanaging. Whatever expectations we have, they should not be exasperating. That is not to say that expectations shouldn't be high, only that they should be age appropriate.

When we define expectations, it helps to have a clear view of the goal in our mind. How do you want your family to be? Is there a picture in your mind? We aim for a strong family, but not a perfect one. That means kids who get along, a happy home, and a good environment for learning. Our aim is *not* to have the most impressive family, or be better than everyone else "because we are Christians." By tempering our goals with realism and humility, we will not be discouraged or deflected from them when things go awry, as from time to time they surely will.

Thresholds

A time to expect challenges is whenever a child is about to cross a major developmental threshold. We would like to comment on four of these thresholds: walking, talking, going to school, and puberty. Anxiety and frustration levels rise at each of these times. When a child is almost walking, but hasn't yet mastered the skill, locomotion can be frustrating. Similarly, when a child's mind understands more than it can express through spoken words, frustration can build. A child can become a bit testy just before the new skill has been mastered. Once walking or talking has become more natural, the frustration level falls. Going to school can also be a time of anxiety. And everyone knows the emotional fluctuations and anxieties associated with adolescence. The point is that at these developmental boundaries, parents need to be extra patient, understanding, and gracious. Anticipating these thresholds helps to keep our expectations in perspective.

Stages

When your child is a baby, what are realistic expectations? Obviously you will not expect a baby to change its own diaper. Nor will you expect it to understand complex instructions. What we can expect is that babies are on a schedule. We can also expect them to be quiet in church and other social gatherings.

If they do become noisy, discretion dictates that we take them to a less public space.

We believe that while basic behavior reinforcement begins as soon as the child is born, real training begins when they are crawling. Since added mobility brings many more objects within their reach, "no" becomes an important command. ("No touch"—i.e., don't touch the stereo, the plant, the electrical socket.) There is no reason we should have to move everything out of baby's path for fear it will create a destructive swath everywhere it crawls. Obviously, remove dangerous or expensive items to a safer location, but there is no need to babyproof or rearrange your whole house just because junior is crawling. The family adapts to the baby, but the baby also must learn to adapt, to be flexible and not insist on its own way. At the toddler stage, there is a superabundance of energy, coupled with a short attention span. Toddling brings even greater mobility—and speed—and it is now even more important that a child show increased responsiveness to parental instruction. Obedience is not optional, nor is this a stage to reason with your child, beyond the most basic level.

Many parents give a child a warning, then begin counting, "One...two...three..." We do not believe this is a good habit, as it teaches the child that it can take its sweet time obeying Mommy and Daddy. Yesterday you may have told your baby girl to come to you, or not to touch the rosebush. Today she appears to be disregarding you, and you are wondering whether she has forgotten what you tried to teach her less than twenty-four hours ago. Don't underestimate your daughter's intelligence, or her memory! No means no, and she understands that short word all too well. It is your job to make sure of it.

Toddlers should also be expected to eat well—no throwing food, fussiness, or flat refusal to eat or taste what is set before them. All three of our toddlers were trained to eat neatly and, more important, *thankfully*. They should also go to bed happily, without protest. They should not be sleeping in their parents' bed. This practice only undermines the children's security by driving a wedge between mother and father, interfering with the sanctity and sexuality of marriage.

Although we trained our girls well to go straight to sleep when it was bedtime, especially when the family had to travel, we had failed to train our son to be flexible. As a result, to this day he still does not sleep as easily when he is away from home.

Training

Training takes time, thought, and patience. Nor is this a one-way street. At family devotionals, as we share in Chapter 17, we occasionally seek input from our children. We have also asked them what they think our New Year's resolutions ought to be! Still, most of the traffic on the street will be flowing from parent to child. Training our children is a mandate of the Lord: *"Fathers, do not exasperate your children; instead, bring them up in the training and instruction of the Lord"* (Ephesians 6:4).

You need child- and family-specific strategies to help the children meet the realistic expectations you have for them. Although they must obey your words, we are looking for more than mere compliance. Recall our discussion of the Rich Young Ruler in Chapter 2. His outward behavior was respectable, but his heart was far from God. This is why we must aim for the heart. In our interactions with our children, are we dealing with the "more important matters" (Matthew 23:23), or minor ones?

Training areas include character, faith in God, attitude, and values like honesty and purity. Other practical areas include money and school (Chapter 21). We must not leave these things to chance.

Training is *proactive*: we act in advance. Discipline, on the other hand, which follows a specific behavior, is more *reactive*. It is concerned with correcting, with modifying behavior.

The more we train our children, the less the need to discipline them. It's up to us. We as the parents choose.

Discipline

Parents can be easily irritated by things their children do and say, and because of our natural tendency to be reactive, we may end up focusing more on small things than on big ones (heart issues). What do you discipline for: pet peeves (like smacking lips) or ungodly character? The following verses really helped us to know where to focus:

> [16]There are six things the LORD hates,
>   seven that are detestable to him:
>   [17]haughty eyes,
>   a lying tongue,
>   hands that shed innocent blood,
>   [18]a heart that devises wicked schemes,
>   feet that are quick to rush into evil,
>   [19]a false witness who pours out lies
>   and a man who stirs up dissension among brothers.
>   (Proverbs 6:16–19)

This must be one of the most useful passages in the entire Bible! The writer explains what *God* detests. If God hates these things, shouldn't we hate them, too? The items in the list are not minor. Table manners and making your bed in the morning do not qualify—not that we shouldn't train our children to be well bred. But the items in this series are matters of character, and in an adult may also be matters of salvation. (You can match each of the seven sins in Proverbs 6:16–19 with these scriptures, respectively: Proverbs 16:5, Revelation 21:8, Revelation 22:15, Genesis 6:5–7, 2 Timothy 3:4, Proverbs 21:28, and Titus 3:10–11.) Let's dissect the passage. It is a reliable guide to the things we should focus on as we correct our children.

1. Haughty eyes

Do your children have "haughty eyes"? When spoken to, do they raise their eyebrows, lower their eyelids, or roll their eyes in disrespect? Disrespect can be shown in many other ways: sarcastic comments, a contemptuous tone, "huffing," and shrugged shoulders. Listen to how they speak to you, to other adults, and to siblings. As parents we need to expect respect from the earliest years. It will certainly be a lot easier to insist on respect when the children are young than to start expecting it when they're already in their teens! It will be easier for our kids to be respectful when they see us interacting respectfully with others (strangers, one another, family members—everybody).

"Please" and "thank you" show respect, and should often be heard in our home. Remember, pride and arrogance are detestable to God. *"All those who are arrogant are an abomination to the Lord; be assured, they will not go unpunished"* (Proverbs 16:5 NRSV). And what God hates, we should hate.

2. A lying tongue

It is common for children and adults to lie. Apart from Christ, who is full of grace and truth (John 1:14, 17), deception and dishonesty prevail. Honesty is one of the most important virtues to train our children in, and lying is a sin that should be taken seriously. As the children get older, when caught in a lie, they may "dig in deeper" if their parents do not give them a way out. Sometimes we would tell our children in mid-explanation, "You won't get in trouble if you tell the truth," or "Before you answer this question, I want you to know that I'm just looking for information. It's not a matter of who did it, or who was right or wrong. Now, who ate all the cookies?" This strategy helps train them to tell the truth, and not to automatically tell an "unnecessary" lie out of fear of punishment.

Relationships cannot be built without love and honesty. Lying destroys relationships and makes a genuine relationship with God impossible. Do your children tell lies? If they do, do you take it as seriously as God does?

3. Hands that shed innocent blood

Though most of our children (hopefully) have not murdered anybody, some children are physically rough. They hit, bite, and bully others into a state of fear. Watch older siblings, who may be intimidating younger ones into not telling the truth about an older brother or sister. All kinds of abusive behavior may go unreported if those being picked on feel threatened.

4. A heart that devises wicked schemes

Some children are furtive and secretive. They will not be open with you, and for good reason. They're scheming! Once again, aim for the heart. Draw them out (Proverbs 20:5), being a good listener (James 1:19). Pray for the Lord to give you insight, and attend closely to your children as you strive to be a more perceptive parent.

5. Feet that are quick to rush into evil

While some people are slow and cautious, others are impusive. We must train our children to deal with their emotions. Impetuosity is not a desirable character trait (Psalm 106:33; 2 Timothy 3:4).

6. A false witness who pours out lies

These words are not just referring to lies, but to lies that get others into trouble. Not all "tattling" is wrong, but lying in order to cause another person harm is a serious matter. See Deuteronomy 19:16–19.

7. A man who stirs up dissension among brothers

Siblings must get along. There are many ways to cause trouble or ill feeling in the family. Watch out for this one!

Share This Scripture!

Share Proverbs 6:16–19 with your children. They will then know that these expectations are from the Lord and not just from you. They need to know who the *real* boss is, the one Mom and Dad answer to. In other words, it's easier to accept discipline as a child when you know your parents are also under authority. Then the kids will hopefully accept that, in your home, you are the boss. In so many families, the children are the ones who set the agenda, tell the parents what to do, and manipulate everything in their own interest. This is the tail wagging the dog.

Punishment

Discipline is not the same thing as corporal punishment, even though many people equate the two. Discipline need not be physical at all, in fact. The chart on the next page displays what we call the four quadrants of discipline. Reinforcements can be positive or negative, physical or nonphysical. Let's move through the four quadrants. Positive physical reinforcements include giving a gift or other reward. Affection itself is a powerful motivator, though we do not believe affection should be withdrawn from an unruly child as a negative reinforcement. Nonphysical varieties of positive reinforcement include a word of praise, or the granting of some privilege. Negative physical reinforcements include spanking or physically requiring the child to stay in time-out (for younger children). Nonphysical reinforcements can be just as effective, and include reprimands and the revocation of certain privileges. (Not the withdrawal of food and water! We are talking about taking away favorite toys, or making the child "unplugged"—no TV, computer, PlayStation, etc.)

A few more explanations are in order. As the children grow older, parents will move increasingly from physical to nonphysical incentives and disincentives. Punishments should be administered promptly and not last too long (not "You're grounded for life!"). Another important thing: If you lose your temper with your kids, be sure to apologize to them. Be humble. This will not diminish your effectiveness as a parent; if anything, it will enhance it. Finally, the goal of discipline is to change behavior, and, at a deeper level, to facilitate a change of heart (attitude, motivation, godliness).

DISCIPLINE

	Physical	Nonphysical
Positive	Gift or other reward	Praise Privilege
Negative	Spanking Time-out	Censure Privilege revoked

Spanking is just one variety of physical negative reinforcement. It is certainly not the chief means of correcting children's behavior, though with most children it is an effective one. The book of Proverbs has much to say about physical discipline, especially in chapter 29:

- The rod of correction imparts wisdom, but a child left to himself disgraces its mother (29:15).

- Discipline your children, and they will give you peace; they will bring delight to your soul (29:17).

- Servants cannot be corrected by mere words; though they understand, they will not respond (29:19).

- If a man pampers his servant from youth, he will bring grief in the end (29:21).

Every year I (Douglas) receive thousands of Bible questions by email. Consider, for example, the following query, typical of the thinking of more and more parents who equate spanking with parental violence:

> My question concerns the practice of spanking children. The word "rod" has many shades of definition in the Bible. The sheep pass under the shepherd's rod in Leviticus 27:32, and it offers comfort in Psalm 23. What is the "rod of men" in 2 Samuel 7:14? In many scriptures, it is described as a tool of measurement. I have two fine boys who learned by consequences but not physical "hurt." What is the message we give them when we "hurt" them physically and we are usually bigger, stronger, more powerful, and hopefully should be more self-controlled?

Here was my response:

> The word "rod"—as well as the word "strokes/floggings" which appears later in the same verse—refers to physical punishment. But you are right: sometimes in the Bible the rod brings comfort, even if at others it brings pain. Either way, the biblical teaching is that the rod brings guidance—and ultimately, security.
>
> It is never right for us humans to physically abuse others, including children. And yet spanking is hardly physical abuse. Of course, some parents are themselves "out of control"—and all attempts to guide their children (verbal or physical, regardless of the incentives tried) end up failing. You underscore a legitimate concern. And yet I believe you may be skirting around some

rather clear passages of Scripture (such as Hebrews 12). This is not to say that children do not respond differently to different rewards and punishments—and yours may be at one end of the spectrum. Most children do not respond to words alone, nor do they have the maturity to learn from mere consequences, especially in the earlier years.

Quite frankly, I would say it is wrong to equate punishment with lack of self-control. For if that is the case, God is the biggest bully out there! We should want our children to learn that there is a bigger, stronger, more powerful being in the universe—and one whom we must obey, for the consequences of failing to do so are dire. Yet some cultures equate spanking with hurt. Life is full of hurt, and such minor hurts can lead small children to respect authority, believe in moral absolutes, and become better persons as a result.

Once again, behavior modification is a far greater enterprise than smacking a child. For some children, there are more effective physical negative reinforcements than spanking. Many parents have learned the benefit of placing their kids in time-out. Our version of time-out was making the rebellious child stand in the corner, without toys or other diversions, back turned to the rest of the household. This worked much better than spanking for our middle child. Our youngest, on the other hand, is quite responsive, and a mere reprimand usually would reduce her to tears. She was more supple and responsive than her older siblings.

"No discipline seems pleasant at the time, but painful. Later on, however, it produces a harvest of righteousness and peace for those who have been trained by it" (Hebrews 12:11). Discipline is not pleasant. That's why children don't like it. Most adults don't like it either, and a growing number want to protect children from any punishment at all. But the benefits of doing it God's way are considerable. Would you like to enjoy the harvest of righteousness and peace? As God's word says, *"Whoever spares the rod hates their children, but the one who loves their children is careful to discipline them"* (Proverbs 13:24).

If you are not sure how to proceed from here, get advice,

but don't become overly dependent on an adviser. The kids will know you got your opinion or latest strategy from someone else.

Conclusion

Training and discipline take time. Strategies will be different from child to child, as every child is different. To be effective, training must be based on ancient, time-tested biblical principles, not modern enlightened ideas of human nature or worldly philosophies (Colossians 2:4, 8).

If we underdiscipline our children, it will be hard for them to obey God, who may be perceived as a threat to their sovereignty. If we overdiscipline, children will project their view of us onto their understanding of God, and probably not want to serve him. Or they may go through the motions, while deep in their hearts they do not believe in or love such a God.

In the final analysis, we cannot force children to become Christians. No one would feel good about the conversion of a child who was told, "Unless you are baptized at church this Sunday, you will be grounded and lose your allowance for the next year"! Conversion must be the child's decision, and this is the subject of our next chapter.

Conversion

Jesus said, "Let the little children come to me, and do not hinder them, for the kingdom of heaven belongs to such as these" (Matthew 19:14).

Several years ago we attended a seminar at which a powerful, dogmatic speech was delivered. The speaker insisted that if a child of Christian parents has reached thirteen years of age and has not yet become a Christian, it is because of sin in the parent's marriage. He was overly confident, and despite a total lack of scriptural support for his theory—not to mention his own tragic family situation—allowed no exceptions.

But how could this man, unknown to many in the audience, know at what age every one of their children and future children would be ready to make Jesus Lord? The Bible, after all, never specifies an "age of accountability." And does the Bible really espouse so mechanical a view of conversion? Does it promise that if your parents are good Christians, the chances are 100% that you will become one, too?

Sure, it would be nice if all children of believers were guaranteed to be automatically converted at age thirteen, and without any chance that they were just going through the motions. That would simplify things, wouldn't it? But this is not reality. All children are not the same. And then there's that troubling, persistent fact: they have free will.

Original Sin in Reverse?

I (Douglas) enjoy fielding questions from around the world that I receive via email, and have been doing this since 1998. This question (from 2005) really made me think:

> It has become a commonplace that if a Christian couple's child doesn't become a Christian, it's because the parents are harboring sin they haven't repented of. But what about Ezekiel 18, where it says the sins of the father will not be on the son, or the son's on the father? This passage even gives an example of a righteous man who has a sinful son. Please help!

And this was my response:

> Certainly a Christian family is likely to turn out Christian kids. Training, parenting, and honoring the Lord in the home are paramount, and there are many scriptures which say as much.
>
> Yet in my view, no, it is not always the parents' fault. Your observation about Ezekiel 18 is on target! Every child has free will. If an unspiritual child always reflects badly on the parent, then what about Eve and Adam? (Was God a bad parent? Does he have "unconfessed sin" in his heart? Of course not!)

I believe that my response validated and encouraged the questioner, yet I felt that I was the one who was learning from the exchange. For many years I had used Ezekiel 18:20 only to show that children do not inherit their parents' sin (the doctrine of original sin). But the sister who emailed me was right: the passage works both ways. Guilt is not directly passed from father to child, nor is it passed from child to father. Following is the key passage. It would be a good idea to read the entire chapter if you are unfamiliar with it.

> [20]The one who sins is the one who will die. The child will not share the guilt of the parent, nor will the parent share the guilt of the child. The righteousness of the righteous will be credited to them, and the wickedness of the wicked will be charged against them (Ezekiel 18:20).

Through Ezekiel the Lord said that the son is not guilty before God for the sin of the father, nor is the father guilty in the sight of God for the sin of the son. Besides, what about God's own progeny: Adam, Eve, and twelve billion others that have lived throughout history? Adam is called the son of God (Luke 3), and generally speaking, all humans "are his children" (Acts 17 NASB). Was the Lord discredited once his children rebelled? The same faulty logic would suggest that Jesus was a bad discipler, since he was unable to keep Judas in the faith.

It seems grossly inconsistent to insist that while the Lord does not override free will, we are assured of influencing our children to become Christians whether or not they themselves are ready to make such a decision.

To this distressed parent I owe the insight that the Ezekiel 18 principle applies to parenting, just as well as to the (wrong-headed) ancient legal practice of punishing a man's descendants even when they are innocent. In reality, the punishment the Bible speaks of—the consequences of family dysfunction and selfishness—is simply the outworking of decisions in the family as they affect, condition, or tempt the children to make their own wrong choices. This cycle of cause and effect can extend several generations, according to the Bible (Exodus 34:7).

It would be odd indeed if Bible believers were unwittingly recreating the doctrine of original sin in reverse! No, the parents are not always responsible for the sins of their children.

What about Proverbs 22?

You may be thinking, "But doesn't God's word promise that if we are good parents, our children will turn out well? Surely if my daughter or son does not become and remain a faithful Christian, it's all my fault." Indeed, many lessons have been preached reassuring us that if we train up our children in the way they should go, when they are old they won't turn from it (Proverbs 22:6). What is wrong with this common teaching?

Proverbs are generalizations about life, not ironclad prom-ises. They are observations, not absolute affirmations. There are two possible translations of this proverb. But even if we adopt the stricter one, we face a big problem. It has to do with the nature of Scripture and how the Proverbs are to be interpreted in the first place.

Leaders of parenting seminars regularly present Proverbs 22:6 as some sort of unconditional promise. This is a mistake. The proverbs sometimes contain unconditional promises, but more often they are general descriptions of reality and admit exceptions. Proverbs 22:6 would support the traditional interpretation (when a child doesn't follow the Lord, it's the parents' fault) only if (1) this passage has been translated correctly—and there is debate on this matter, (2) the passage covers the entire period from childhood to old age—which is far from clear, and (3) the promise is unconditional.

The Nature of Proverbs, Adages, and Maxims

Proverbs, adages, and maxims do not attempt to offer comprehensive truth about any one subject. They are generalizations. Consider the twin English proverbs: *He who hesitates is lost. / Look before you leap.* Both are true! They are complementary, not exclusive. Someone who lives exclusively by either one of these adages will become one-sided, the first landing in many troubles through rashness, the second languishing in an overconservative paralysis. Neither saying contains the whole truth of the matter, which concerns how long to wait before making decisions. So it is with the biblical proverbs.

For a biblical example, consider Proverbs 23:21. It reads, *"Drunkards and gluttons become poor, and drowsiness clothes them in rags."* This is a general truth; there are exceptions. There do exist rich people in the world who are also alcoholics and gluttons. Proverbs 16:3 reads, *"Commit to the Lord whatever you do, and your plans will succeed."* This is another general promise. Sure, when we are seeking God's will, things tend to go better than when we aren't. But we cannot manipulate God. Nor can we commit our children to the Lord with absolute certainty that they will stay with Christ.

Case by Case

Proverbs 22:6 has been misunderstood and frequently mistaught. If the proverb is a general observation, a principle, this means that even a godly man or a godly couple may end up having one or more children who reject their parents' faith. Of course, if these children are persistently wild, rebellious, or disrespectful, a prospective elder is disqualified (1 Timothy 3:4–5; Titus 1:6). That's because if a man cannot manage his own household, how will he manage the church? (Note: Translations reading "faithful children" or "trustworthy children" are to be preferred over those that read "believing children." But that discussion is beyond the scope of this book.)

We believe it is wiser to consider each situation case by case, instead of jumping to conclusions about the parents when one or more of their children have rejected the faith. Of course, it would be great if every child responded in faith and repentance to the gospel. After all, this is God's expressed will (1 Timothy 2:4). But not all do, and we cannot control what happens, only contribute to the outcome. Which situation do you think would reflect better on a child's upbringing: a family in which one child out of one became a Christian, or a larger family in which six out of seven children responded to the gospel? Is the question hard to answer without knowing the children and the parents? Exactly our point. Reason, love, and prudence dictate that we should consider each family *case by case.*

Controlling Outcomes

Some of you may be thinking that we are covering up our own bad parenting by embracing such a "liberal" position. As parents of Christian children, let us assure you that we have no desire to lower the bar of Christian parenting by implying that how one's children turn out is unrelated to the parenting they received during their years at home. Far from it! All we are saying is that, in our zeal to manage outcomes and people, we may put parents under tremendous pressure. (Not to mention their children.) Some parents have been ostracized, even publicly humiliated, because one of their kids "struggled," quit the faith, or did not choose Jesus as Lord. This is tragic, and not godly. Where wrong principles have been taught, it behooves us to change the way we think.

The goal of Christian relationships is to show Christ to the people of the world (2 Corinthians 2:14), not to manipulate them or even necessarily to change them. It is up to the Lord to open their hearts (Acts 16:14; 2 Timothy 2:25–26). The difference between the two—showing Christ and influencing another person to change opinions or behavior in response to him—is not a mere nuance. There is an ocean of difference between be-friending someone to get him to join your group and sharing the love of Christ unconditionally. Jesus died, after all, for all of us, not just for those who would be saved. So it is with parenting.

If this is a difficult concept, allow an analogy to throw light on the subject. What is the goal of sports? Is it only to win? Of course not. Vicki and I are the sort of people who still believe, "It's not whether you win or lose, but how you play the game." To think otherwise is to ill prepare children for a world in which everything seldom goes one's own way.

We must even ask, what is the purpose of being a Christian? Some claim the entire point of being a Christian is to make other people change so that they too will become Christians. But is this really biblical? Beyond doubt the mission of a follower of Jesus Christ is to have an impact in this world—to help the needy and to reach the lost. But mission and purpose are not the same thing. Our *purpose* as Christians is to know God and to bring him glory (John 17:3). It is to be close to the Lord and to enjoy our relationship with him, not to "measure up." Of course, obedience to his commands is not optional, nor is the Great Commission of Matthew 28:19–20. The Lord expects a return on his investment in us, as scores of scriptures make clear.

Our purpose is to spend eternity with God in a relation-ship of faith and love. Our *mission*, on the other hand, is to be the light of the world, to make a difference. Yet, sadly, when Christians think their purpose is only one thing, be it helping the poor, knowing the Bible well, or saving the lost, they lose balance, perspective, and joy. Perhaps one year they don't suc-ceed in helping someone directly to become a Christian, and as a result they feel like failures. Some are even threatened with scriptures promising that the "unfruitful" will be cut off from the vine and burned. In John 15:1–17, the passage being alluded to, fruitfulness is simply productivity. It cannot be measured solely in terms of numbers of persons saved, sacrifices made, or hours in prayer. God expects obedience, and this is part of our being his true followers. But never should this be equated with our purpose.

Indeed, confusion about our purpose creates unhealthy pressures and patterns. Confusion about parenting—such as arises when a mother or father imagines the only parenting responsibility is influencing a child to become a Christian—may lead children to dark places. Each child will have to make his or her own decision. How do you feel about this statement? Helpless? Powerless? Disenfranchised? Or does it help you focus on what you *can* do?

Of course we want our children to make Jesus Lord in their own lives, but if our love for them is conditional on their making that choice, something is seriously wrong. That's because that is not how God loves us. He allows us to bear the consequences of our choices, yet he still continues to do all he can to draw us closer to himself.

The Age of Accountability

Parents email me their questions about children and conversion: "When are children ready to make their own decision?" "When are they ready to be baptized?" "When should the kids become Christians?" Parents ask these questions because they care, because they are uncertain or insecure, and certainly because they sense the magnitude of what is at stake. The bottom line answer: God knows. And in one way, the answer is academic anyway. If they jump the gun and "take the plunge" too young, they will—we trust—figure this out later in life and "do it right." On the other hand, if they are dilatory, or are not eager and willing to take this step of faith, then God knows they are not truly prepared—and no amount of prodding can change this reality. We must accept what the Lord gives us, while continuing to pray that one day their hearts will be opened.

But surely, for some, this is an unsatisfying answer. You may be wondering, "What is the 'age of accountability'?" Since Jesus was twelve when he was becoming deeply aware spiritually (Luke 2), is this the magic age? "Tell us the answer!" you are tempted to plead. All we can do is to share our opinion. Many, if not most, twelve-year-olds are not as mature as Jesus was, at least in spiritual terms. Many *are* ready by the time they reach fourteen or fifteen, and perhaps earlier if they are advanced or have a solid spiritual foundation. By the same token, some may not be ready until their later teens. Who can say? (Only God!) There comes a point in time at which, like Eve and Adam, our children's eyes are open (Genesis 3:5, 22). They have deliberately done what they know to be wrong. Their sin is premeditated. Exposure to sin and temptation comes in different ways to different children. Some children experience the depths of evil early on in their lives (drugs, gangs, rape). Others may never experience such horrors. It seems reasonable to conclude that exposure to sin and temptation, provided the child does what is wrong with open eyes, may accelerate his "accountability" in the eyes of the Lord.

Although it is not easy for us parents, we must "let" our children be lost. A drowning man cannot be rescued before he has fallen into the river. Don't be surprised if your children get involved in sin. Although they have the power to resist, they don't. The trespass is a necessary step on the way to salvation. Perhaps it is out of insecurity that we want to nail down the exact age at which our sons and daughters are "ready." But this we must leave to the Lord. Like us, they must come to faith and repent. They will be learning and growing before this point in time, and they will certainly not have finished growing anytime soon after conversion—any more than we have! The promise of salvation in Christ and the promise of the life-changing Spirit are for all generations. All must "obey the gospel" (2 Thessalonians 1:8; Acts 2:38–39), and our children are no exception.

To paraphrase Paul's exhortation to Agrippa, short time or long—I pray to God that all will make the decision to follow the Lord (Acts 26:29). And so with our children. Short time or long, the important thing is *that* they arrive, not so much *when* they arrive.

What Can We Do?

In the words of Frederick Douglass, "It is easier to build

strong children than to repair broken men." The Bible has much to say about how to bring up our children so that they make their own decision to follow Christ. To cite the familiar Deuteronomy 6 once again:

> [5]Love the Lord your God with all your heart and with all your soul and with all your strength. [6]These commandments that I give you today are to be upon your hearts. [7]Impress them on your children. Talk about them when you sit at home and when you walk along the road, when you lie down and when you get up. [8]Tie them symbols on your hands and bind them on your foreheads. [9]Write them on the doorframes of your houses and on your gates (Deuteronomy 6:5–9).

It all begins with our own commitment to God (verse 5). This commitment must be sincere (verse 6). God's word is to be in our hearts and unquestioningly followed. That is why we will need to take the time to impress it on our children (verse 7). Example alone will not do it; Bible teaching is necessary (and vice versa). This is not the responsibility of the children's ministry of the church. It is the responsibility of the parents. And all of this will involve much discussion and many, many reminders (verses 8–9).

But although we must leave outcomes to God, there are many practical steps we can take. Here are a few suggestions:

- Husbands and wives, pray together daily! Vicki and I ask groups wherever we go to speak if they are doing this simple thing. We have observed that, in most places, not one man in twenty is praying with his wife on a daily basis. Prayer brings you closer as couples, leads to resolution of differences (Ephesians 4:26), and forges the unified front which is crucial for the children's security and own personal faith.

- Teach your children to have daily devotions, or "quiet times," even from a young age. They need not be long—the length and depth of the devotions will depend on the child's age, maturity, and interest level. We started our children around the time they entered school. Others will begin earlier, or later. If they begin at a young age, by the time they are entering the teenage years, it should have become a habit.

- Read excellent books on parenting, marriage, and family. Why reinvent the wheel? Learn from others. Make it your custom to take advantage of the many resources available. (The resources section at the end of this book features helpful parenting books, periodicals, and websites.)

- Leave home for church on time so that there is no sense of rushing. Poor planning sends the message that church is a low priority, compared to, say, going to work or being on time for a movie or concert.

- Cooperate with your local children's ministry workers. When they offer feedback on your children, do not be a "fool" (Proverbs 12:15, 18:2, 20:3, 23:9, 28:26). Be quick to believe the reports of your children's teachers—whether at church or in school—as well as babysitters. (Why do so many parents bristle at feedback meant to help them with their little darlings?)

- Talk about the word of God in a variety of settings (Deuteronomy 6:7–9). Share with your children from your own Bible study. They will be "impressed."

Is this merely a list of rules? We hope not. These are only ideas that have worked for us and for others. You and your spouse need to discuss the matter, come to agreement, and work together on any changes you would like to make. Whatever strategy you devise, remember that the goal is to impress God's commands on the *hearts* of your children.

What Does It Take?

We have talked about issues of control, accountability, and responsibility. But what does it take for a child to become a true Christian? The short answer: nothing more or less than it takes an adult to be converted. Here are some things we have found useful to focus on when younger persons want to follow Jesus Christ:

1. Your child should be developing a personal relationship with the Lord. It is not theoretical, but increasingly a daily reality.

2. Your child should be reading and interacting with the Scriptures. When you show him/her something from the Bible, there is a humility, flexibility, and willingness to make changes without arguing.

3. In all likelihood, your child will be asking more and more questions about the faith. There may be "Bible contradiction" questions, queries about the justice of God, science questions, etc. A good evidences book may make a difference.

4. It is natural, when faith is becoming real, that the individual wants to share with others what he has been learning. Although it is difficult to say *how* evangelistic we should expect a maturing child to be, sharing one's faith is an essential element in coming to Christ, who bids us all come, follow him, and go out to gather with him (Luke 11:23). Your child will be reaching out to schoolmates and other friends, and sharing what he/she has been learning.

5. Your child will invariably begin to build closer relationships with other children who are living for Jesus Christ. His/her closest friends should not be only those "in the world"—not that it's wrong to have non-Christian friends—but also among the community of faith. New friendships take time to develop. This cannot be rushed or forced.

6. Do *not* expect your child to emotionally advance to the maturity level of a twenty- or thirty-year-old. All children still need to go through the various stages of maturation, whether Christian or not. (Just as they will still be growing physically.) You should, however, expect them to take responsibility for their actions and spiritual lives.

7. Sin must be specifically acknowledged and repented of. Apathy, disrespect, laziness, deceit, self-centeredness, and other heart sins will, in many cases, be more prominent than the sins of the flesh (sexual sin and other worldly activities).

A Word to Single Parents

Some of you are single parents, and we recognize that your situation presents some special challenges. It may be harder to help your children come to faith. Since single parents have to do the work of two, extra patience is required. The two-parent family is God's ideal, yet thousands of committed, vibrant disciples of Jesus Christ have been raised by single parents. In other words, as challenging as your situation is, never accept the lie that the obstacles are insurmountable. Here are some practical ideas:

- Pray daily with your children. When possible, join with another family for devotionals.

- If remarriage is a possibility, pray for it patiently. Don't let frustration affect your judgment.

- Beware the temptation of letting TV become a babysitter. Instead, encourage your kids to invest in friendships, sports, schoolwork, chores, and reading. Do you really want advertisers and overly liberal programmers conforming your children to the pattern of this age? (Romans 12:2).

- Do not grow too close to grumblers and complainers, whose negativity may influence you (Proverbs 22:24–25; 1 Corinthians 15:33). The world is filled with people who will offer you a false sympathy, one that fosters a critical spirit rather than a Christlike one. Form your closest friendships with faithful, positive Christians.

- When you take your younger children to church and drop them off in children's ministry, make sure they have a positive, giving spirit *before* they go to class. Once again, cooperate with teachers, accepting their feedback.

- Remember, character issues are of the essence, more than external behavior. Focus on the heart (Proverbs 4:23).

- Finally, when you are tired—perhaps after a long day—don't "tune out" when your kids need you. Yes, they need you to go "one more lap." You are serving as both mother and father to them!

A Word to Spouses of Nonbelievers

Sometimes parenting and family life become extra complicated when one parent decides to follow Christ and the other does not. In one sense, though this is not the optimal situation, it is hardly surprising. After all, the Lord himself said, *"Do not suppose that I have come to bring peace to the earth. I did not come to bring peace, but a sword. For I have come to [divide]"* (Matthew 10:34–35).

If this is your situation, do not despair. Whether you are a man or a woman, the principles of 1 Peter 3:1–6 apply:

> [1]Wives, in the same way be submissive to your husbands so that, if any of them do not believe the word, they may be won over without words by the behavior of their wives, [2]when they see the purity and reverence of your lives. [3]Your beauty should not come from outward adornment, such as braided hair and the wearing of gold jewelry and fine clothes. [4]Instead, it should be that of your inner self, the unfading beauty of a gentle and quiet spirit, which is of great worth in God's sight. [5]For this is the way the holy women of the past who put their hope in God used to make themselves beautiful. They were submissive to their own husbands, [6]like Sarah, who obeyed Abraham and called him her master. You are her daughters if you do what is right and do not give way to fear.

This passage teaches that, in winning over your mate, your character is more decisive than your words. A few practicals:

- Be humble and submissive, focusing on the qualities of your inner spiritual life.

- Resist the temptation to make subtle "digs" at your mate, whether in direct conversation or in your prayers. This is unlikely to help your children to become Christians. Pray for a gracious spirit. (The Proverbs will prove faithful friends!)

- In the same vein, when you speak about your spouse to others, be positive. Remember, he/she does not have a "voice"; your brothers and sisters in Christ are likely forming their impressions of your mate through your words. Never, ever speak ill of your spouse in the presence of your children. This could undermine their respect for *you!*

- Strive to coordinate schedules, giving advance notice whenever possible. Sometimes this means that when there have been sudden changes in plan (e.g. the last-minute prayer meeting or church party), you will need to stand at your spouse's side.

- Avoid arguing with or raising your voice at your spouse, or losing your temper. Your mature example in Christ, not childishness, will help to change his/her heart.

- When you do sin, be quick to confess and ask for forgiveness both from your spouse and from your children. Show them that you know you need God's grace and are grateful for it.

Conclusion

All of us want the best for our children. While ultimately it is up to God, not us, to touch their hearts and move them to conversion, there is still much that we can do to create an environment conducive to faith. Though we are not the ones in control, we can pray for God to help us model what we believe, help us see past our blind spots, and move through his Spirit to create faith in the hearts of our sons and daughters.

Certainly there is no joy like the joy of seeing one's child come to Christ. That joy rarely comes without a cost. We have a great responsibility to our children. Are you ready to do your part to meet that cost?

Adoption

Religion that is pure and undefiled before God, the Father, is this: to care for orphans and widows in their distress, and to keep oneself unstained by the world (James 1:27 NRSV).

In ancient times taking care of one's own immediate family was assumed. The Scriptures frequently speak of the widow, the orphan, or the fatherless, and those who had lost their living relations and were in need of a family and the protection of a home. The practice of taking in orphans and widows was not a given, however, and in the event no living relatives were present to assume their traditional and honor-bound duty, these needy persons would be at the mercy of an uncaring world. That is why God so often tells us through the Scriptures to take care of the helpless, those truly alone in the world. The terms "orphan(s)" and "fatherless" are mentioned forty-five times in the Bible. A typical passage is Isaiah 1:17: *"Learn to do good; seek justice, rescue the oppressed, defend the orphan, plead for the widow"* (NRSV).

Adopting Our Daughter

Although there are many other ways to support bereaved children besides adoption, some families decide to take the huge step of adopting an extra family member. In August 1994 Douglas and I "finally" decided to adopt, and in April 1995 we traveled to Shanghai to collect our youngest daughter. Persevering through the process developed our characters and also piqued our desire to see our new toddler and bring her home. (Thirteen years later, in April 2008, we returned with Lily to her place of abandonment, and to her orphanage. Though not her first return to China, it was her first time back in Shanghai. Naturally, emotions were not in short supply!)

We were all able to set eyes on each other, as a new family of five, at my mother's house in England. She had looked after James and Emma during our trip to China. It was the Easter holidays. What an emotional moment it was, a reunion that was the response to months of prayer and longing! The instant Lily and James met, their eyes locked. They smiled and bonded right away. This was her big brother (James was six). Emma, on the other hand, was a little reticent. She was happy but over-whelmed, and asked my mother, "Can you cry happy tears?" At four she was overjoyed to meet her new sister, but it took a little longer to bond. Emma was no longer the baby of the family, and she struggled with jealousy. This was hard for her, as one-year-old Lily was now getting *all* the attention.

We discussed with Emma that it was okay to feel jealous, but we needed to be honest and talk about it. We also explained that it was *not* okay to hit Lily or pull her hair. You may need to have the same discussions if you are adding a child to your family by adoption—just as you would if the new addition were born to you directly. Truthfully, it took about eighteen months to get to the point that all three relationships were equally strong.

Parenting in All Three Dimensions

Up to the point when we adopted Lily, parenting had seemed black and white, rather two-dimensional. (Just feed them and take them to church and—presto—out comes fami-ly.) Adopting a child has caused us to parent differently. It has called us higher and enriched the family immeasurably. With adopted children, there is a much greater need for attention, affection, and affirmation. New feelings had surfaced, and now as parents we had to deal with emotional needs far more than we ever had before.

Lily's life was blessed by God, but ours even more so. We began to parent emotionally—as we learned to anticipate deep-felt needs. We all became a lot more affectionate and encouraging as we needed to secure this family. Our "square" of four family members had become a "circle" of five. Our family has been "completed" by God for over two decades now. Many of our discussions have moved away from the "black and white" into the gray: feelings, emotions, the uncharted psychological waters. From time to time, Lily needed to talk about the deep issues, or else she began to grow anxious. As Proverbs 20:5 says, *"The purposes of a man's heart are deep waters, but a man of understanding draws them out."* One issue was her sense of loss, not knowing why—why her parents couldn't take care of her. She also wanted to know what her "other" family looked like. There were no answers we could give her, nor do the authorities in Shanghai have any information about this. Only God knows.

When she was younger, she would often ask, "Are you coming back?" She had been "left" once before, and deep inside she dreaded being alone again. And for an adopted child, there is always the subsurface fear of being rejected, which emerges at school and in social interactions.

Adopted children are *not* the same as other kids. The issue of abandonment, which is a real one whether or not they knew their previous parents, cannot be ignored. It colors so many things in their lives.

Our adopted daughter is a most affectionate child, with a captivating laugh and smile, and an appreciation for the way God has taken care of her. We are grateful that she has taught us to be three-dimensional parents, dealing with physical, spiritual, and *emotional* needs.

Get Ready to Learn!

As disciples of Jesus Christ we are called to be students, to be learners. Adopting a child means you will need to learn fast. Plan to read many books. A great deal of useful material has appeared in print since we adopted our daughter. We believe that parenting is learning to meet your children's needs beyond your own.

Should We Adopt?

Adoption is not for everyone. But if you have the spiritual and financial means to bring in a child who needs a family, you will be blessed by God. If you have done all your research, including talking with other adoptive families to learn from their experiences, perhaps all you need to do now is to *decide to decide.* Don't delay any longer. There are tens of millions of orphans in the world: war orphans, AIDS orphans, and others. There are tens of millions of other children who need to be placed in loving, functional families. Might it be that God is calling you to bring one of these children into your family?

Conclusion

Adopted kids have their own special issues. To meet their needs and keep maturing emotionally ourselves, we must learn to parent in all three dimensions: physical, spiritual, and emotional.

In the fifth section of the book, "Rhythms," we will discuss the events that punctuate family life and give it consistency: mealtimes, traditions, and family devotionals. One additional chapter will address life's transitions that disrupt the normal rhythms a secure home life enjoys.

V

Rhythms

Mealtimes

They broke bread in their homes and ate together with glad and sincere hearts (Acts 2:46b).

Separate Lives

Before we had children, Douglas and I were living in Sydney, Australia. One month, we became part of a "sponsored fast," organized to raise money for the poor. We emptied out our refrigerator and watered down the fruit juices (so we wouldn't be tempted). And then we cut out all food and mealtimes for over a week.

In seven days I lost seven pounds—not that we were trying to lose—but in ten days of fasting Douglas lost twenty-five pounds, and many times became lightheaded. When he preached, he often slurred his words. (It was quite humorous, in a pathetic sort of way.) It took him two years to put all the weight back on! We sent Douglas out into the neighborhood to collect the sponsorship money, because he looked so gaunt and thin.

What really struck us during the whole experience was not our different metabolic rates, but that during the fast we never sat down together. We were so busy, even busier than normal, as there was no need for a meal to slow us down. We were going our separate ways. We were like strangers, crabby and hungry but raising money for the poor. We were united in our mission, but not in our relationship. In the language of Acts 2:46, we were sincere, but not glad!

The same sort of thing can happen to all our families. We become so busy that we are reduced to eating fast food in the car as we drive from one event to another. Is your minivan literally "meals on wheels"? Meals are an essential part of the Christian life. Don't miss out on the opportunity to build family around the table.

Mealtimes Are Prime Times

How important are mealtimes, food, fellowship, and just sitting down together? How many times in the New Testament do we see Jesus Christ eating with people, creating family as he taught others? God has created us to need food and fellowship, to rest and relax, and to be fed. We must slow down and enjoy mealtimes and see them as part of God's plan for family.

Maybe you don't like cooking, but you surely desire to serve your family a nutritious meal, to help them thrive, to provide for them. It is worth the sacrifice. Meals can be simple. (You will find some ideas later on in this chapter.) But it takes planning and deciding that dinner time is an essential part of family life, and in all likelihood you, as the mother, will be the one to take the responsibility. After all the preparation, the food can be gone in minutes—especially if there are hungry teenagers around the table! If dinner is only about the food, it will bring the family together physically, but not necessarily emotionally.

For this reason, after dinner we like to play a game for twenty or thirty minutes. We tend to get hooked on one game for a month or two, and then switch to another. Favorites include Yahtzee, Monopoly, Canasta, Backgammon, Scrabble, and Clue. (Our family is also quite fond of crossword puzzles.) On the other hand, if it is family devotional night, we normally start it thirty minutes after the meal, to allow time for the washing up.

Don't Let Anything Crowd Them Out!

Fight for family mealtimes even in the high school years. Rearrange schedules and limit afterschool activities so that there is time for family meals. Our goal once the kids started school was to have breakfast and dinner together daily. This became a constant for us. Were there occasional exceptions?

Sure. It didn't always happen that we managed two meals a day together, but we always had at least one.

Breakfasting together is a wonderful way to start the day. I (Vicki) took responsibility for it, and it became earlier and earlier each year as school started earlier for the children. We would get the younger kids up earlier to fit in with the older ones' schedules. It is great to know that the kids are happy and not hassled, fed and not fed up as they leave for school, and encouraged as they leave home on cold, dark mornings. While it would have been more convenient to send the girls to school on the bus, that would have meant thirty minutes less time together. So to make breakfast happen, I needed to be willing to drive them to school for a few years. This meant less time for "my things," but more time for family, and also more time for the kids to read and pray before leaving for school.

Advance Preparation

Make family meals rather than buying them. You do have the time, and you will save a lot of money. You may have to give up a TV show in order to plan for the next day, or you may need to prepare a week's worth of meals at a time if you work outside the house. Buy a new cookbook or go online to get fresh ideas. Go for the thirty-minute dinner. You can include your kids in choosing the meal and cooking it. Teach the older kids to cook, using only four or five ingredients, and this will revolutionize your family life. It will also train them for the future.

Talk!

Talk around the table. Switch the TV off and don't answer the phone during family time! Make this time encouraging, keeping correction out of the dinner hour if possible, or else the kids will dread mealtimes. Most of our meals end in mirth about the day's mistakes. We like to joke and make one another laugh. This is a time to share, to catch up, and to encourage.

Family Event

Mealtimes were a family event when the kids were growing up. Lily set the table, Emma loaded the dishwasher. I cooked and cleaned up the cooking mess, and James was the trash master—and catalyst for most of the humor. Douglas made the after-dinner tea. We were usually able to make him slow down and sit down (no computer or phone) for a good twenty to thirty minutes! The cook sets the tone for this meal. It is a wonderful way to serve your family. We need to give and we need to be needed as parents. Gratitude flows from the family when we prepare and serve the family meal. The dinner table is a place where people talk and where the "real you" comes out, because it cannot be hidden. We learn so much about our children when we take the time not just to eat with them, but to listen to them and enter their world.

Crunch Times
Yes, we had "crunch times"—nights when we were going to activities or church, chaotic times—but we still needed to eat. But fast food was a rare treat, not a staple. Here are some fun ideas for meals:

- Toasted sandwiches. These are a cinch to make.
- Eggs and toast, prepared to order.
- Chili & chips (oven fries) and salad. Chili can be from a can or thrown together simply using ground beef, onion, a can of tomatoes with chili seasoning, and a can of red kidney beans or black beans. While the oven fries cook, prepare the chili. This takes no longer than 20 minutes.
- Breakfast again. A typical Sunday evening can feature breakfast foods, especially pancakes. This is easy!
- Buttered spaghetti pasta with black pepper and parmesan. This takes 15 minutes.
- Soup & salad with crusty bread. (Get the kids to make the salad.)
- Use a slow cooker (one pot meals) while at Sunday church—another timesaver.

We would like to make one more suggestion. If you are

a family that has food delivered (for example, pizza), still sit around the table and eat it together. Don't separate, each heading to a private world inaccessible to the rest. Mealtimes integrate the family. Perhaps this is one reason the Scriptures emphasize them so much.

Healthy Meals

Our world is overdosing on fast food. These days, most schools, under pressure from the fast food industry and its allies, have stopped serving nutritious meals. It is sad to see so many overweight kids in America, and even back in England child waistlines are ballooning. There is less and less exercise in schools. Parents need to respond by changing the kids' diets, and of course by encouraging physical activity. (More on this in chapter 21.)

Cut back on snacks, or cut them out entirely. While snacking is part of American culture, it is an expensive and not always healthy habit. Another great idea is to serve water. Usually the kids are thirsty, and it is easy for them to become dehydrated. Water *and* juice, or water and milk, is a good way to go. When we go to restaurants, the family normally orders water.

If you take this advice, you will save on your food bill. But the real gain is the value of the time together, not the money saved.

But I Hate to Cook!

We all have our pet "hates." (Mine is ironing.) Yet part of being a mother is sacrifice. The best way I know to create family and fulfill many desires is a home-cooked meal. I know some of us hate to cook. But it's hard to be a mother without being a cook. (I didn't say "gourmet chef"!)

Whom Do You Really Thank?

Yes, we encourage the children to appreciate the hard work that goes into preparing tasty meals. But whom do we really thank? In 1 Timothy 4:4 the apostle Paul says, *"For everything God created is good, and nothing is to be rejected if it is received with thanksgiving, because it is consecrated by the word of God and prayer."* This is the prayer of thanks. In fact, every meal recorded in the New Testament is preceded by a prayer of thanks—even the meal amid the storm that shipwrecked Paul and company! (Acts 27). Our custom is to return thanks before every meal. The children gave thanks even when they were at school. God is God, whether we are at home, in church, at work or at school, and we ought to honor him at all times. (No, there was no big announcement when the kids prayed at school, usually just a quiet prayer, although sometimes tables of children prayed together, especially in the part of the country where we live, where things are exceptionally religious.) We believe these are wholesome habits to form in our children, as in ourselves.

- Though our family shared breakfast and dinner nearly every day (school prevented family lunches on weekdays), occasionally we ate out. Even then, praying before the meal was routine.

- The Lord said we will not necessarily be heard because of our "many words." Most of our table prayers are short and to the point.

- Many toddlers learn to pray by repeating the exact words of a parent. Like many of you, we started out this way with our kids.

- In our family, each member took a weekday. Daddy led the prayers on Monday. Mummy (British spelling!) took Tuesday. Our eldest (when home from college) took Wednesday, our middle child Thursday, and the youngest child Friday. Everyone knew when everyone else's day was. At weekends we were more flexible.

Is this your practice? Sadly, many professing Christians do not pray before meals—so how can they expect their children to pray and grow in gratitude, returning thanks to God? Once again, whom do we thank for meeting all our needs?

The Predictor

Why is it that some boys and girls grow up to be responsible, moral, and contributing members of society, while others never reach their potential? What would you guess that people who are unable to hold down a job, struggle with depression and suicidal thoughts, drop out of school, suffer divorce, surrender to obesity, give in to alcoholism or drug dependency, or even end up in jail all have in common? The experts have carefully researched why some kids turn out well while others end up as underachievers or delinquents.

Numerous studies have all come to the same conclusion. During their formative years, while children were still at home with their parents, the family did not take time to sit down at the dinner table on a daily basis. On the other hand, those whose families made mealtimes a priority tended to form in their children a healthy sense of self-worth, strong values, an ability to bond relationally with others, and perseverance through tough times.

- In a 2005 *Wall Street Journal* article, "Much Depends on Dinner," it was reported, "These days, fewer than one-third of all children sit down to eat dinner with both parents on any given night... The decline in the family dinner has been blamed for the rise in obesity, drug abuse, behavioral problems, promiscuity, poor school performance, illegal file sharing and a host of other ills."

- The BBC ran a news feature on Britain's teenagers, acknowledged by all to be ill behaved. It too concluded that the best (and only consistent) predictor of healthy adjustment is the family mealtime.

- A study at Harvard Medical School concluded that the odds of being overweight were 15% lower among those who ate dinner with their family on "most days" or "every day" compared with those who ate with their family "never" or on "some days."

- The National Center on Addiction and Substance Abuse at Columbia University found that teens from families that almost never eat dinner together are 72% more likely to use illegal drugs, cigarettes, and alcohol than the average teen and that those who eat dinner with their parents fewer than three times a week are four times more likely to smoke cigarettes, three times more likely to smoke marijuana, and twice as likely to drink as those who eat dinner with their parents at least six times a week.

- A 1995 Heritage Foundation study convincingly disputed the notion that race is a prime issue in crime. "A closer look at the data shows that the real variable is not race but family structure and all that it implies in commitment and love between adults... Most delinquents are children who have been abandoned by their fathers and are often deprived of the love and affection they need from their mothers." Did you get that? *Structure* is good. And the rhythm of mealtimes is one of the most obvious features of family commitment.

The mealtime is "the predictor"! These times create and help maintain the integrity of the family unit. Let them go, and the family literally dis-integrates.

God's word was right all along. Mealtimes serve a vital purpose in the development of your children. Do not underestimate the vital function these family times serve.

Traditions

Every year his parents went to Jerusalem for the Feast of the Passover. When he was twelve years old, they went up to the Feast, according to the custom (Luke 2:41-42).

Several times a year, according to the Old Testament, all the Jews were to converge on Jerusalem, the holy city (Deuteronomy 16:16): *"Three times a year all your men must appear before the Lord your God at the place he will choose: at the Feast of Unleavened Bread, the Feast of Weeks and the Feast of Tabernacles."* Though we will not go into the details about the celebrations and memories afforded by these mandated "conference times," they were integral to the cohesiveness of the nation, socially, politically, and spiritually. At Passover, Pentecost, and the Feast of Tabernacles, every Jewish adult male was expected in Jerusalem. Women were exempted so that they could take care of their children. (Is there a lesson somewhere in there for us?) Of course, as the children got older, or when other adults volunteered to help with the family, many women and children did attend these grand events. It is just such an occasion where we find Jesus and his other family members in Luke 2.

Imagine the excitement of going up to Jerusalem! The focal point of one's entire life was the temple and its priesthood. This was not just an overnight trip. The journey itself to the holy city would have taken a number of days. And the time spent traveling as a family (assuming the children were old enough) would have been a true pilgrimage. To walk up the steep ascent to Jerusalem, immerse oneself in a ritual bath before entering the temple courts, and then offer a sacrifice to God, mingling with thousands of other pilgrims who had come from all over Israel—how exhilarating this would have been! It would have made a deep impression on a young boy or girl. Nor was the trip to Jerusalem for the Feast of Passover wasted on the child Jesus (Luke 2).

The Bible is full of accounts of personal and national revival taking place during these holy days of Israel. (See, for example, the books of Ezra and Nehemiah, in which we read of times of refreshing as the people of God renewed their commitment.)

Holidays

How can we take advantage of holidays and the other occasional "downtimes" to create family, make memories, and be refreshed spiritually? The word "holiday" came from *holy* + *day*, and theoretically, at least, holidays were to be times of special devotion to God. And yet we have observed the "vacation paradox": when people are on vacation ("holiday" in British English), spirituality quite often plummets. The more free time we have, the more difficult it seems to "fit in" God, make time to read and pray, and capitalize on the occasion. Here are a few practical suggestions:

- Prepare spiritually before your vacation. Do not be haphazard. Plan to read, pray, and grow during this time. Take along a good spiritual book to read, perhaps one a friend has recommended to you.

- Go on holiday with another family, especially one whose children are friends with your children. We have fond memories of trips with dear friends to such places as Niagara Falls, Maine, Hong Kong, England's Peak District, Krakatau (Indonesia), and the Outer Banks.

- Enjoy the great outdoors. Marvel at God's creation. This has the potential of creating and reinforcing faith in children—not to mention us!

- A Christian conference can be a great way to spend a long weekend, school break, or summer holiday time.

- Take a vacation to the third world. Let the children see how most of the world lives. It will make them much more grateful for what they have.

- Don't become a "martyr" and try to do it all when having family or friends come to your home. Get the whole family involved in the preparations. Too many mothers are more exhausted at the end of their "vacation" than at the beginning. (Fathers and any children reading this book: Don't let this happen. Pull your weight!)

- Instead of going away, have a vacation out of your own home. Save on hotel expenses! Eat out some, eat in some, do some special things. Plan some interesting day trips. There are several benefits: You'll spend much less than you would if you traveled away from home. There is also less anxiety, since you know where you are and how everything works. Best of all, you get to sleep in your own bed!

- Keep in mind that, for some, holidays can be sad times. People remember departed loved ones who are absent from the celebration. As Christians, we should be sensitive to this.

- Finally, don't live for summer vacation or Christmas. If you do, you will probably be disappointed. Live during the rest of the year, and you will continue to enjoy the abundant life during the special times, too!

Building Family Traditions

Traditions are customs we follow that are not required by law, commanded by God, or necessitated by our living conditions. Traditions are not necessarily bad; the only ones Jesus criticized were those that violate the word of God (Matthew 15; Mark 7).

Traditions embody who we are, and everybody has them— every nation, culture, company, and family. Every family has its own set of traditions, and needs them. They help to define who your family is, what you believe in, and what you consider important. Since every family is different, the following ideas (some of our family traditions) are only to stimulate thinking, not necessarily to be copied—unless they really appeal to you and your children.

- Sunday night, have breakfast. (In our house, this was one of the few meals that father cooked!)
- If your kids make something artistic, put it up on display. Our laundry room was a gallery for pictures our girls painted.
- Write notes and put them in your kids' lunchboxes. This encourages the kids, especially if the school day is a rough one.
- I (Douglas) make tea in the morning and serve it to Vicki in bed. (She loves that!)
- Once a year, take away each child on an overnight parent-child trip.
- Encourage your children to make creative gifts. We encouraged our kids to make presents and cards for each other at birthdays and Christmas, instead of buying them from stores. For example, our son, James, is not gifted in the arts and crafts department, but he is a wonderful poet. He writes poems of appreciation; this is his way of expressing himself. They are marvelous keepsakes.
- Our daughter Lily loved to make baked goods as her gifts, and this became a common mother-daughter activity.
- Don't try to make up for your mistakes as a parent by buying big gifts. Money doesn't buy forgiveness. Books make good presents, as do games and DVDs, things the whole family can share.
- Make car rides to church fun, not hurried. Sing on the way, or listen to worship music. Play family games in the car. As a side note, if you're running late for church, don't blame the kids! The tension before church can be awful, and so ungodly. We are the parents; the problem is *our* lack of planning. Get organized!
- Be international. For example, during the American

Thanksgiving holiday, we combine cultures when we select foods to prepare (a British trifle, or a pumpkin cheesecake, even Chinese food). Be adventurous.

- One of our birthday traditions is that the one whose birthday it is chooses the dinner for the family. And it can be anything! It is our tradition to serve the meal to the birthday person on a large, red plate.

- Birthdays can be great for family sharing times, each member expressing what he or she appreciates about the birthday boy or girl.

- Consider "unbirthday presents," an idea especially helpful for younger kids. The tradition came from the British side of the family. It originated because on Vicki's twin sisters' birthday, she received nothing while they received everything—or so it seemed. Vicki's mother decided that every child would receive a present—just one.

- Sometimes on the way home from Wednesday night church, we would stop and pick up French fries.

Whereas holidays are rare, coming only so many times a year, traditions can be observed year round. What are your family's traditions? Chances are, when they are grown up, your children will continue many of them, and even your grandchildren will perpetuate the family traditions.

"Dates"

If you're the father of a little girl, let me strongly urge you to set aside a weekly time for a "date" with her. Two of our three children are girls, and they both savored their "dates" with Daddy. I took out my younger daughter for a snack after school every Monday. My older daughter and I went out to breakfast on the way to school every Thursday.

Were there exceptions to the schedule? Sometimes. But we nearly always managed to get our "dates" in. This is a time to talk, to listen, and just enjoy being together. It's a special father-daughter outing. We enjoyed our "dates" for quite a few years, and I am sure our girls—regardless of their age—will always remember them. So will yours.

In addition, when our son is in town, he likes to be taken out for breakfast and a prayer in the park. Sometimes I will take out a child to a restaurant for a special dinner, just the two of us.

It may be less necessary for mothers to have scheduled time with each child, as they tend to spend more time with the children in a variety of settings anyway (homework, driving them to activities, and so forth).

Christmas

Although Christmas is not a biblical holiday—it was not mandated until centuries after Christ—it is still part of the ambient culture for many of us. So many people celebrate *Christmas* without appreciating *Christ.* They may try to drown their sorrows in eggnog or yuletide shopping. And worse, they start the new year fatigued, overweight, and in debt! How can we as Christians capitalize on the season, so that it isn't a dead loss spiritually? A few special Christmas suggestions:

- Watch *A Christmas Carol.* This film moves the heart. If there is a real "spirit of Christmas," this is it!

- Visit the sick in hospital. We will never forget the Christmas we took our family on a visit to the geriatric ward of a local hospital.

- Bring dinner to a poor family.

- In Sweden, where we lived for several years, people open presents on December 24. Some years we like to follow the Swedish tradition.

- Enjoy an "Advent calendar."

- Sing Christmas carols together as a family.

- Don't go into debt, buying presents you cannot afford. A less expensive Christmas may be more special than an elaborate one. This is so important that a separate section will be devoted to it.

Christmas Wisdom

In many Western families (those who are part of Western culture—not those living in Wyoming or the Yukon), Christmas is a time of multiple gifts, given in every conceivable permutation and combination. (Each family member, nuclear and extended, gives a separate gift to every other family member.) The number of presents can be enormous, and the appreciation level for all involved may not be where it ought to be. Sensory overload! (And credit card overload?)

Well, many years ago we started consolidating, simplifying, and saving a lot of money. Rather than a Christmas tree with scores of presents underneath, we focused more on the Christmas stockings. We realize that for some of our readers what we are saying is culturally foreign, but perhaps there will be a helpful nugget somewhere in this suggestion! We bought one family gift for all. That is, each family member did not go out and buy a gift for every other family member. The one family gift was for everybody to share. One year it was an annual membership in the Baltimore Aquarium. Another time it was a Christmas trip to Disney. Once we bought a trampoline—yes, a family present! Another family Christmas present was a puppy. Yet another year the family present was a visit to serve the poor in a third-world nation. (All those frequent flyer miles came in handy!)

No, the individual stockings were not stuffed with lumps of coal; we did spend money on the stocking gifts—in some years, more than we did on the family present. Also, the stocking gifts were wrapped, so it did take a little time for everyone to open them. (Of course, some relatives and friends gave us gifts, which went under the tree—so it wasn't completely bare under the lower boughs!)

The result of this more thrifty approach:

- The kids were more grateful than they might be with "present overload."
- Christmas was still fun.
- We never had to pay off holiday debts in January. This also made it a cinch to be consistent in giving financially to the

work of the church. Is this perhaps an idea worth considering for your own family?

Conclusion

Holidays, birthdays, and Christmas need not be "dead" times. If we plan and prepare, they can become moments of spiritual growth and drawing close to the Lord for the whole family. Family traditions are valuable, not only in defining who we are, but also in building unity and connection.

Devotions

> Let the words I enjoin on you today stay in your heart. You shall tell them to your children, and keep on telling them, when you are sitting at home, when you are out and about, when you are lying down and when you are standing up (Deuteronomy 6:6-7 NJB).

Family devotions, or devotionals, are times when the family comes together and "devotes" itself to worship, Bible study, and spiritual growth. They can take place at any time convenient for the family, as frequently as you think best, and wherever you want them to, and they can last as long as you like. There are no rules, though we will share a few ideas later in the chapter. Devotionals are a direct implementation of the principles of Deuteronomy 6—taking advantage of opportunities to talk about the Lord and his word with one's children.

With this in mind, we encourage you to have devotionals, or the equivalent. Do you have regular times of spiritual learning and encouragement with your family? According to the Bible, this is God's plan for our children's spiritual upbringing. Whose responsibility is it to make sure this is taking place? The head of the household is responsible.

These should be fun, learning times (Ephesians 6:4), but it is also important that the kids see your devotion to God. How ironic if your devotionals were fun family times, but not spiritual ones! We as parents are charged with the sacred trust of bringing up our children in the instruction of the Lord.

There are many teaching opportunities throughout the week: mealtimes, at bedtime, during walks around the neighborhood, drives, etc. Don't limit your spiritual interaction and discussion to the devotional—any more than you would want to limit your Christian fellowship to the Sunday service. Spiritual interaction is an ongoing, daily happening. Why not take your child on a "prayer walk" with you? Or maybe you can read the same book of the Bible together in your morning devotions. Should you do a "quiet time" with your children every morning? Whatever your decision, remember that ultimately it must be their faith, not yours, that impels them to become Christians. Let their faith grow naturally. Nurture it. Share a quiet time with them if they have the appetite and interest, but give them room to grow!

Never underestimate the impact of your faith on your children. To illustrate, one young man shared in front of the congregation at a Father's Day service about his parents, and how even when his dad traveled away on business, he and his wife would pray together for thirty minutes on the phone. The son saw their everyday devotion to God, not just once a week in a devotional setting. It was obvious to us that it touched him deeply. It motivated him personally to be close to the Lord. Our spirituality, or lack of it, registers with our children. They are perceptive, and they are also teachable. Let's teach them by actions, not just words.

How Often?

As new parents, we were advised to have daily family devotionals when James, our first, was two and a half years old, and Emma was not even walking. We failed! This schedule was too rigid for us, and we constantly felt guilty, so we aimed for two devotionals a week. For us, that was just right for the toddler stage.

We vividly remember a devotional with our firstborn, James, about Noah and the ark. We took it from *The Beginner's Bible,* when honestly he was too young to understand the stories. At the end, Douglas asked him, "What did Noah do when it started to rain?" James happily responded, "Oh, Daddy, he put up his umbrella." We tried hard not to burst out laughing, but with tears coming down our faces from the force of the suppressed laughter, we quickly ended the devotional and began to question what we were doing. The humorous event led us to a change in approach. Devotionals became a time for a few songs and a prayer together for a while! The lessons grew with the ability of the children to appreciate them.

So how often should we have devotionals? Every week, or every day? Every family is different, and you will need to make your own decision. We prefer to wisely abstain from legislating. If pressed to give an answer, and replying in the words of Jesus (1 Corinthians 11:25 NASB), we would say, "As often as you do it."

What Should We Do?

In your devotional, sing songs, pray, teach the Bible, and talk. Answer the kids' questions. Meet needs, make it fun, and tie it in with what the children are going through in their lives. We found that from toddlers to older teens, everybody likes devotionals. Let the kids lead some of the songs and prayers. Occasionally, we even let them prepare the lesson. (This became increasingly easy as they entered the middle school and high school years.)

Sometimes only one adult will be present. Time and again, women ask, "What should I do if my spouse isn't participating?" Mothers, you can do the "devo" if Dad is out of town or unable to be there. Perhaps he is not a Christian, or is having a hard time spiritually. If this is the case, choose a time for the devotional that doesn't embarrass or humiliate him.

Devotional Ideas

It's always nice to "steal" ideas that work from other families. Here are a few of ours:

- Work your way through a gospel, covering a chapter or so each time you are together. Prepare well and be ready to answer the kids' questions.

- Find an encouraging proverb that applies to the person on your left; go around the circle. Everybody shares.

- Share what you are reading in your own personal study. Everyone discusses what he or she is learning.

- If you prefer to hold devotionals on a daily basis, you might begin each weekday with a "thought for the day." We did this for a whole year. With three children, every family member had a weekday to share a verse (usually from Psalms or Proverbs). Immediately after breakfast, and before everyone had risen from the table, the thought was presented and discussed. (We went in descending order of age, just for fun.)

- On a poster board, draw a map of the Mediterranean world. Follow Paul on his missionary journeys (starting in Acts 13). In each devotional, trace the next segment of his journey with a marker, writing directly on the map. Everyone will learn, as history, geography, and the Bible come to life.

- If your kids are old enough to be in the service with you, discuss the Sunday sermon.

- Tape the name of a biblical figure onto the back of a family member. Everyone else can see who he/she is. Questions with yes or no answers allow the individual to find out his/her identity. Instead of a person, this might be a place, or even the devil. (Our kids especially loved to try to "stump Daddy.")

- Hold an open question time. This can be very faith building, and allows the children to be honest about their thoughts, including their doubts.

- For larger families (three or more children), have the kids write a spiritual skit and act it out. This is not only entertaining; it builds family spirit and makes concrete the spiritual principles the family is focusing on.

- Conduct a "Rant, Rave, or Repent" session—an idea we "stole" from friends in Seattle. Here's how it works: Anyone may speak. A "rant" is a complaint or strong suggestion for someone else in the group, voiced to that person directly. This is an implementation of Matthew 5:23–24 and 18:15. A "rave" is the opposite: you share positively about someone else—something that person has done, or a significant change seen in his or her life. A "repent" is a decision you have made and want to share with the family. "R-R-R," as we sometimes called it, is not just for the kids. Everyone shares in it! Thus the family learns that devotional is a safe place to talk. We held "R-R-R" at the end of about a third of our family devotionals.

Do you need more ideas? Why not buy a book of family devotionals? See the resources section at the end of this book, or search our website.

Conclusion

Family devotionals implement the principles of Deuteronomy 6 and Ephesians 6. They bring the family together, provide a "safe" place to talk about spiritual things, and foster real Christian growth. They work!

Transitions

For we walk by faith, not by sight (2 Corinthians 5:7 NAB).

As we have discussed in the previous chapters, mealtimes, traditions, and devotions mark time in the flow of family life. Their cadences become familiar, and together create a sense of normalcy. But there are many things that disrupt the rhythms of family life.

The Purpose of this Chapter

In this chapter we will consider seven such events: *moving, starting school, losing a job, death, additions to the family, leaving home,* and *traveling parents.* The purpose of the study is to equip us to bring our children through these times with a minimum of disruption. What enables our children—and us—to do well through these times of transition is living by faith, not by sight (2 Corinthians 5:7). In other words, the faith of the parents directly influences the children. The stronger and the more consistent the adults' faith, the easier it is for the family to avoid what would otherwise become tumultuous, turbulent, testing times.

1. Moving

From time to time your family may need to move. In our increasingly mobile society, most of us will change residence many times. Some of you reading this have moved ten or twenty times in as many years! Even if it all goes smoothly, moving is still a highly disruptive, potentially traumatic experience. This is doubly true for children, especially when they are school age. In the Bible, we read of many families that had to relocate for one reason or another. One well-known example is the family of Abraham, who left Ur, a prosperous urban center, and migrated to the promised land. *"[Abram] took his wife Sarai, his nephew Lot, all the possessions they had accumulated and the people they had acquired in Haran, and they set out for the land of Canaan, and they arrived there"* (Genesis 12:5). Like Abr[ah]am, we need to be faithful, going where we believe God wants us to serve him. Our faith sculpts and sustains a sense of security for our families. It is so easy for us to become attached to earthly possessions, especially our homes! Our materialistic society has whispered many lies into our ears. How much better it would be to drink deeply of the pilgrim spirit commended in Hebrews 11, where we read:

> [8]It was by faith that Abraham obeyed when God called him to leave home and go to another land that God would give him as his inheritance. He went without knowing where he was going. [9]And even when he reached the land God promised him, he lived there by faith—for he was like a foreigner, living in a tent… [10]Abraham did this because he was confidently looking forward to a city with eternal foundations, a city designed and built by God (Hebrews 11:8–10 NLT).

Even when Abraham reached the place to which God had called him (Genesis 12:5), he still did not put his trust in his new home. Like him, we look forward to a city with eternal foundations. It does not exist anywhere on this earth.

Referring to Abraham and others who exhibited this faithful pilgrim spirit, the Hebrew writer continues:

> [13]All these faithful ones died without receiving what God had promised them, but they saw it all from a distance and welcomed the promises of God. They agreed that they were no more than foreigners and nomads here on earth. [14]And obviously

people who talk like that are looking forward to a country they can call their own. [15]If they had meant the country they came from, they would have found a way to go back. [16]But they were looking for a better place, a heavenly homeland. That is why God is not ashamed to be called their God, for he has prepared a heavenly city for them…

[39]All of these people we have mentioned received God's approval because of their faith, yet none of them received all that God had promised (Hebrews 11:13–16, 39 NLT).

The high velocities of our society have spoiled us. Jet travel, express mail, fast food, quick mortgages, rapid transit, electronic tax filing, and the lightning-fast worldwide web—and we dearly love them all! They all reinforce the illusion that everything can (and should) happen when we want it to. Yet we need to learn to wait, to be patient, and to be still (Psalm 46:10). We also need to be good sports even if we don't receive what we want when we want it. The spiritual world is not an on-demand society. Its values are vastly different from those of the material world, as we will soon explore in Section VI.

When it is time to move, put your faith in the Lord. Be patient. Moving takes a lot of time and energy—that part is unavoidable. If it is not an earthshaking, angst-producing event for you, neither is it likely to be for the kids. They respond to your faith and look to you for confidence. Here are some key principles:

- Don't become too fond of the things of this world, including your home.

- Search the Internet for a moving timeline and a moving checklist—there are some excellent ones. Good planning and preparation diminish the sense of chaos surrounding moves.

- Pray as a family for the details and smoothness of the move.

- Talk about the Lord and what exciting things he may be planning for your family in the new community to which you are moving.

- Remember where your true citizenship is, and where your ultimate home lies. Keep walking by faith, not by sight!

2. Starting School

For many parents, the start of school for their five- or six-year-olds is a major trauma. We have seen parents weeping because of the "loss" they feel as their kids advance to the next stage of childhood. One wonders whether all the to-do is stemming from the child, or from the parent! Here are some thoughts:

- Always speak positively about school. Never speak negatively or project fears onto your child. For all intents and purposes, your attitude determines your child's attitude about starting school, whether enthusiastic or apprehensive.

- Pray *about* the new situation, and pray *through* any fears your child may have expressed.

- The Lord will help our children grow up and will strengthen them when they need to be "brave." They, and you, must walk by faith, not by sight!

3. Losing a Job

In our fast-changing corporate world, it is more and more common for companies to downsize. Employees are laid off, and not always because of poor job performance. Such a transition can constitute a crisis in family life. We know what it is like to lose our jobs. This happened to both of us in 2003. At the time, we had just moved to Sydney, with financing from our employers guaranteed for one to two years. A few weeks after relocating the entire family to Australia, we were informed that support could no longer be provided. We weren't "fired," but the effect was similar. We now had two decisions to make: which country to move to (we have both US and UK residency), and which direction to go in terms of employment. After twenty years with one "company" (a church), we decided to go in an independent, freelance direction. This quickly became an exciting, exhilarating time. What was God doing? Where would he have us live, and what would be different in our lives?

Our main concern was that the children see our faith and consistency through this time of transition. And they did. Here are some strong suggestions for you if your transition is the loss of a job. (Note: We are not talking about retired persons, but those of the age and ability to work a regular job.)

- Pray. Stay sharp spiritually. Refuse to cut back on your personal devotional times.

- It is generally more difficult for an unemployed person to do well spiritually than one with a job (2 Thessalonians 3:6–12). Losing a job is not the prelude to an extended vacation. It is simply a transition, and one that more and more people are having to go through. Prepare yourself to work harder, to take it higher. Your children are watching and learning.

- Be sure to express gratitude for your previous job and employer. Gratitude is a quality you want your children to embody, not negativity, complaining, or bitterness.

- Work *hard* until you find another job. Until that time, your full-time job is to look for a full-time job. Don't sleep in. Get up and seek until you find.

- Loss of a job calls on the entire family to keep walking by faith, not by sight!

4. Death

Of course death presents a major transition for the one who has died, but here we are concerned with the effect on the children. Perhaps a grandparent has died. Or maybe a sibling has passed away. While we may be tempted to minimize or avoid talking about the tragedy of what has happened, this is not right.

In biblical culture, mourning was public, and the period of mourning was protracted. When Stephen died (Acts 7:60), the book of Acts says that *"godly men buried Stephen and mourned deeply for him"* (Acts 8:2). They did not minimize the loss by saying, "Stephen was saved when he died; we should be rejoicing instead of weeping." Yes, Stephen had nothing to fear; paradise awaited him. But no, this does not mean that others experienced no loss. They suffered emotionally because they loved Stephen. He had been part of their life, but was so no more. Another example may be found in Acts 9:39, with the (first!) death of Dorcas.

In modern Western society, on the other hand, we are acutely uncomfortable with death (Hebrews 2:15). And, because of our discomfort, our children suffer. We have a valid need to get our feelings out, and our children need not be shielded from the reality of what has happened. Instead, we must help them prepare to face their new reality and enable them to process this emotionally.

We all deal with grief in different ways. Women tend to be able to deal with it straightaway, while men take longer. We also all process grief at different rates. It is important not to judge someone according to your own feelings or manner of grieving. As Proverbs 14:10 says, *"Each heart knows its own bitterness."* Take special care not to impose your own opinions about grieving onto others.

- Do not euphemize. ("Grandma has gone on a long trip," or "Uncle has gone to meet his father.") Be honest.

- Answer directly and honestly any questions the kids may ask, though with responses appropriate for the age of the child. Speak clearly and simply.

- Make sure you are talking about your own feelings, processing your own grief. Pray to God and share what you are dealing with (1 Peter 5:7). That will enable you to speak to your children appropriately, without importing your own emotional baggage and rendering yourself incapable of meeting their needs.

- If the person who died was in the immediate family (parent or sibling, or a relation who had lived with the family for a long time), the sense of loss will be especially acute. Do not hold back; it's fine to cry. Give the family opportunities to talk about their grief and weep, and also about the good things they appreciated about the departed one.

- Certain times of the year are likely to be hard for children: Christmas or other traditional family times, the birthday of the deceased, the anniversary of the death, and so forth. These need not be depressive occasions, though heavy feelings should not necessarily be discouraged. They can, rather, be times of remembering the dead in a positive way.

- For adopted children, death can be a reminder to them of their own loss. Maybe their parents died, or they were abandoned. When I (Douglas) lost my father, we were surprised how hard his death hit Lily, our adopted daughter, even though they were not particularly close emotionally. Again, when a distant cousin lost a parent (whom Lily had never even met), she was the most affected. Adoption creates certain empathies otherwise not to be expected. The old sense of abandonment is again awakened, and adopted children are grieving silently over the loss of their birth parents, making these transitions even tougher on them.

- "Celebrate" the life of the person who died. Perhaps plant a tree, or let each family member buy a Christmas ornament that helps them remember your loved one. One year on the anniversary of my sister's death, I (Douglas) drove to a town between our home in the Washington DC area and my mother's home in Florida. We brought photo albums, cards, and other keepsakes, and talked for hours about someone we dearly missed (my sister, who died at age twenty of diabetes).

- By dealing with death forthrightly and spiritually, you as parents will enable the entire family to "move on," despite the fact that things will never be quite the same. It's all about faith.

5. Additions to the Family

Whether your family is growing by the birth of another child, the addition of an adopted or foster child or a stepchild, or even a relative moving in with you, previous family dynamics are affected. This too is the kind of transition that has the potential to be a source of great blessing or extreme disruption for the family. Good preparation makes the change easier for your children:

- Rethink schedules, chores, and responsibilities to integrate the entire family. Everyone will have to adjust in order to "make room" for the newcomer. Of course, the most important place to make room is in our own hearts (2 Corinthians 7:2).

- Get the children praying for the new addition. For example, six months before we adopted Lily, our other two were praying for her daily. Once she joined us, it was a homecoming as much as the start of something completely new. Within no time it was hard for any of us to imagine a period when she was not part of the family.

- Seek advice from others who have successfully gone through the same transition.

- See the resources listed at the end of this book that apply to your situation; included are books on adoption and a "For Blended Families" section.

- Keep walking by faith, not by sight!

6. Leaving Home

When a child leaves home, for example to attend university, a gaping hole is left in the family. There is, and should be, a sense of loss. Another issue is that, even though launching children is what parenting is all about, controlling parents can make it hard for the child to actually "leave." Parents want to be needed. Yet at such times, the way parents can best help is sometimes not to help, not to interfere.

- Stay in contact with your adult children, but allow space for them to develop their own lives apart from you.

- Do not underestimate their continued need for their parents—they still need direction from you!—or their need to make their own decisions, even to goof up from time to time.

- Pray through your own emotional issues. This is a time during which parents should mature, not just children.

- If your own parents are still alive, this might be a good time to speak to them about how they handled your own leaving home. Bring them into the discussion; they will feel honored.

- Keep walking by faith, not by sight!

7. Traveling Parents

In Old Testament times, all the men were required to travel to Jerusalem three times a year (Deuteronomy 16:16). These were big trips, and often the wives and children stayed home. (Though not always—see Luke 2:41–42.) In modern times, it is not that different. We were once serving at an event at our son's school, when the topic of conversation turned to traveling husbands. We were shocked! It seemed every woman we spoke to had a husband who spent a number of days a month away from the home on business. We are not unique.

Both of us used to travel a lot, but we noticed that this became harder on the kids as they grew older. They needed more stability, so Vicki increasingly stayed at home. Her travel schedule dropped to only a fraction of what it used to be. On the other hand, my (Douglas') travel schedule has hardly changed since the early 1990s except for a few years when our kids needed me home more, as discussed below.

I would like to share some things we have learned. Consider Paul's longing for his spiritual "family": *"You long to see us, just as we also long to see you"* (1 Thessalonians 3:6d). And how about Proverbs 25:25? *"Like cold water to a weary soul is good news from a distant land."* The family wants two things when we travel. First, since fundamentally they want us—to be connected to us—they need to know that we miss them, and that their relationship with us is very important to us (not just to them). The other thing they want is news. What did we do when we were away? What was it like?

As the kids get older (approaching and in the teen years), the impact of our absence or presence is even greater. In many families, it would be wise to cut back or even eliminate travel completely. For the sake of our family, it became necessary for me to pare down the travel schedule. Not only were the kids happy about this, but Vicki was thrilled! In other situations this may not be necessary; every family is different. So many fathers (especially) are "not there" for their children because of their travel schedules. And others may, technically speaking, never leave the home, but they "travel" emotionally. How can we be sure we are staying connected with our families during these times of absence?

- Phone your spouse as often as you can. This has an impact on your children, even if you are not able to speak with them. It shows your love as a couple, and establishes the "ladder" of relationship priorities so integral to a stable home life. Phone home during layovers. Phone home from your cell phone on board the plane before takeoff and once you've landed, when permissible.

- While phoning is best, it is not always feasible. Emailing the kids is easy and fun. These days, many private homes and most hotels have Internet connections. Many cities also have Internet cafés, and more and more hotels worldwide have wireless Internet. (My wife especially loves to get a beefy email, especially when I'm sharing my observations and feelings.)

- Mail a letter from home before you leave. The family (or family member) will then receive it a day or so after your departure (a nice touch). A postcard is also a colorful and easy way to stay in contact.

- Husbands, arrange to send your wife flowers—making sure they arrive after your departure.

- Life usually gets busier, not easier, when one partner is away. When you return, don't expect that everything in the home has been done or has gone as smoothly as it would have if you had been there. Be gracious.

- Bring back small gifts (even if just the packet of jam from the hotel breakfast!).

- Prepare to be giving when you return from a trip, since the others are waiting for the report, and are eager to see you. Even if you have traveled twenty-four hours from the other side of the world, be energetic when you walk through that door!

- Not traveling at all is the best option for many families. Although marriage can still be good even through periods of separation, and the kids may manage well, this is not always the case with every family. For some, travel—even in small quantities—it is not a good idea.

- Men should also consider the issue of sexual purity. Many, if not most, men away from home for extended periods are tempted with hotel cable television, female business associates, drinking, etc. Since there is less "accountability" away from one's spouse, reporting back to a strong Christian while you are away is a wholesome practice. Another idea: Don't turn on the TV in the hotel room—ever. Be wise.

- Take control of your own travel arrangements, if this is possible. Check potential engagements against family events, so that family truly comes first. For this reason, I always book my own travel.

- When you travel, take the Lord with you.

Conclusion

Faith is the key to dealing with disruptions that come into our lives and put pressure on the family rhythms that would otherwise provide us with a sense of normalcy and peace. Times of transition will also require lots of discussion. Talking things through—dealing with issues—also helps us to see more clearly the hand of God in circumstances. Faith allows flexibility and room for God's Spirit to move and change us through every time of transition.

In the final section of the book, "Values," we will examine the subject of Christian values: materialism, caring for the poor, the media, fitness, money, and education.

VI
Values

Virtue vs. Values

They are from the world and therefore speak from the viewpoint of the world, and the world listens to them (1 John 4:5).

The world is too much with us; late and soon,
Getting and spending, we lay waste our powers:
Little we see in Nature that is ours. —*Wordsworth*

Before exploring worldly and Christian values, we probably ought to define terms. First, what is meant by "worldly"? Is it necessarily bad to be familiar with the world, "street smart," or a friend of tax collectors and sinners? Of course not! In the New Testament the phrase "the world" usually refers to life apart from God, and the system of sin, self, and independence from the Creator that the ruler of this world promotes (1 John 2:15). In John 3:16 and other passages the more familiar meaning of "the world" is found: human society. So in the latter sense we ought to love the world, yet in the former sense we ought *not* to.

The other term to define is "values." In the old days people spoke of virtue. "Virtue" comes from the Latin for *valor, manliness, excellence, courage, character, worth.* Its basic meaning is *moral excellence.*

Yet today it seems all talk of morals, good, and evil is suspect. Today the world prefers the term "values." What you value—your preferences about right and wrong—are your values. They may be "true for you," but not necessarily "true for me." This is the essence of *moral relativism.*

Diametric and Diabolical Opposition

The two systems are in competition. God's way is true, good, pure, and right. The enemy's way is false, evil, impure, and very wrong. The first way centers on heaven and others, the second on the world and self. The first is a narrow and difficult way; the second, broad and comfortable. One constitutes a small minority, the other a huge majority. Although people can cross over freely from one to the other, there will come a day when this is no longer possible (Psalm 1:1–6). At that time, the two ways will be revealed for what they really are, for the blinding brilliance of the Lord himself will bring everything to light.

Accidental Adultery?

Even though many passages in God's word refer to the two systems, it is easy for us to forget. The home is meant to be a haven, a place of protection against the pounding of the world at the doors of our family. Yet if we are off our guard, the world will come through that door, or enter at some other point of access. When it does, we have lost our Christian distinctiveness. The low calling of the world is then substituted for the high calling of Jesus Christ, and love of the world eclipses our true, first love (Revelation 2:4). That is why the Lord warns us:

> [4]You adulterous people, don't you know that friendship with the world is hatred toward God? Anyone who chooses to be a friend of the world becomes an enemy of God. [5]Or do you think Scripture says without reason that the spirit he caused to live in us envies intensely? (James 4:4–5).

God will brook no rivals, any more than you would accept your husband or wife having another spouse "on the side." In the Bible, both testaments repeatedly warn us that admiring, flirting with, and having a relationship with the world is tantamount to spiritual adultery. But don't most Christians "blend in," especially in societies that claim, nominally at least, to be Christian? Are their lifestyles really any different from those of their non-Christian neighbors, workmates, schoolmates, or family members? What about "the salt of the earth," the light of the world," and "the city on a hill"? (Matthew 5:13–14). Why is it that Christians can so easily accommodate themselves to the other system? "The world is too much with us," as the English poet Wordsworth wrote. The apostle John explains the dangers:

> [15]Do not love the world or anything in the world. If anyone loves the world, the love of the Father is not in him. [16]For everything in the world—the cravings of sinful man, the lust of his eyes and the boasting of what he has and does—comes not from the Father but from the world. [17]The world and its desires pass away, but the man who does the will of God lives forever (1 John 2:15–17).

It's not the world in the abstract that tempts us. Who, presented with the option to say no to Jesus Christ, follow the crowd, compromise morals, lose idealism, and one day, totally unprepared, meet a holy God in judgment, would agree to it? But the tempter doesn't tell the whole story. He doesn't want us "reading the fine print." His angle of approach is *"the cravings of sinful man, the lust of his eyes and the boasting of what he has and does."* He knows we are weak in our flesh, even if the spirit is willing, and he will do anything to take our minds off heaven, our eyes off the cross, and our focus off living for the one who died for us.

All the World's My Stage

The father of lies (John 8:44) wants me to believe that, in my personal drama, I am the major character on the stage, and all others are minor characters, or "extras." Even Jesus Christ is a minor character, according to the prince of darkness. Further, he convinces us that self is the center of the universe, morality is judged on a sliding scale, and religion is only to be tolerated in moderation. In fact, the lord of this world has all of humanity under his control (1 John 5:19). His realm is "the dominion of darkness" (Colossians 1:13).

The evil one counsels moderation and tolerance. He doesn't mind if we follow Christ—provided it's only for a short distance. He doesn't object if we read the Bible—but just a few minutes now and then, so that we don't truly understand its message. He's even fine with our going to church and being religious— provided we don't make the sharp break with the world required by the Master.

> [14]Do not be yoked together with unbelievers. For what do righteousness and wickedness have in common? Or what fellowship can light have with darkness? [15]What harmony is there between Christ and Belial? What does a believer have in common with an unbeliever? [16]What agreement is there between the temple of God and idols? For we are the temple of the living God. As God has said: "I will live with them and walk among them, and I will be their God, and they will be my people."
>
> [17]"Therefore come out from them and be separate, says the Lord.
>
> Touch no unclean thing, and I will receive you."
>
> [18]"I will be a Father to you, and you will be my sons and daughters, says the Lord Almighty."
>
> [7:1]Since we have these promises, dear friends, let us purify ourselves from everything that contaminates body and spirit, perfecting holiness out of reverence for God (2 Corinthians 6:14–7:1).

The Lord commands separation from the world, not accommodation. And yet simply acknowledging this fact is not enough. We must actually *choose* one system or the other (Deuteronomy 30:19; Joshua 24:15; 2 Corinthians 6:17). And then we must move: away from the world and towards Jesus Christ, or away from Jesus Christ and closer to the world.

Evidence of a Struggle?

Do our children know about the two systems? Do they know about the lies on which the world system is founded? More important, do they see their parents in combat with the powers of evil, resisting the domination of the adversary? Does the Holy Spirit seem real to our sons and daughters, real because of his reality in our lives? Do they sense the true power that animates their father, their mother? And if they did, wouldn't that arrest their attention—at the same time intriguing, alarming, worrying, comforting, challenging, ennobling, motivating, and inspiring them?

The evil one is a moral burglar, stealthily attempting to break into our homes. In all too many homes there has clearly been a "break-in," but "no evidence of a struggle." Not just individuals and families, but entire congregations have bought into the values of this world. Let's get specific:

Marks of the World

How do we know which value system is ours? It's no big mystery. What did the Master teach? Comparing worldly values with Christian ideals, we quickly perceive the stark contrast. We see that there can be no compromise.

1. Materialism

Our treasure is in heaven, not on this earth (Matthew 6:19–20). But the world values the material too highly. It is more than materialistic; consumerism has a chokehold on the world. Consumerism has been defined as "living to consume, and consuming to live." Its legacy is emptiness (1 Peter 1:18). The essence of consumerism is earning, spending, and getting. It's acquiring things ("stuff") and keeping up with the Joneses (Ecclesiastes 4:4).

Materialism is also dehumanizing. "Net worth" is defined solely as your *monetary worth*. If you aren't affluent, you're worth little. If you're rich, you're valuable, worth something. If you're living in poverty, you virtually don't exist.

This is clearly at odds with everything God tells us in his word. Instead of loving people and using things, we have been conditioned to love things and use people. Nowhere is this more true than in the United States, which though only constituting 5% of the world's population, consumes some 70% of its resources. When love of this world has us in its "vice grip," our concern for the needy recedes into the posterior chambers of our consciousness (and conscience).

And what about the biblical imperative to help the needy? (Galatians 2:10, etc.). In both the Old Testament and New Testament we are encouraged time and time again to remember the poor. Of the scores of passages dealing with the subject, our family has been deeply convicted by such verses as Deuteronomy 15:4–5, 11; Job 31:16–23; Isaiah 58:6–10; Amos 6:1a, 4–7; and the piercing oracle of Ezekiel 16:49–50. The Proverbs have also spoken loud and clear to us (3:27–28, 14:31, 19:17, 21:13, 28:27, 30:7–9, 31:8–9). But this isn't only an Old Testament doctrine. Luke, with his emphasis on poverty and wealth, shouts loudest among the New Testament writers (Luke 3:10–11, 6:20b, 6:24–25a, 6:30–31, 35, 10:25–37, 12:33–34, 16:19–24). Acts, Luke's second volume, continues the theme (2:44–45, 4:32–35, 6:1–7, 11:27–30, 9:36, 10:1–2, 4b…). And then there are all those passages in the letters, like James 2:14–26 and Galatians 2:10. A passage that speaks with perfect clarity is Luke 10:25–37, otherwise known as the Parable of the Good Samaritan.

When you and the children have convictions in this important area, you can donate books, clothes, and other goods to charity. Do it as a family! Regularly support worthy charities financially. It's good for your heart and it helps to cultivate character in your sons and daughters.

Materialism hurts people, but that's not all. It is destroying our environment. What about the ecological responsibility inherent in the first command given to mankind? Genesis 1:28 reads, *"God said to them, 'Be fruitful and multiply, and fill the earth and subdue it; and have dominion over the fish of the sea and over the birds of the air and over every living thing that moves upon the earth'"* (NRSV). But materialistic philosophy views the earth and people alike, as objects to be used and discarded. Truly, consumerism is the bane of our culture. But Jesus said, *"Watch out! Be on your guard against all kinds of greed; a man's life does not consist in the abundance of his possessions"* (Luke 12:15). How we earn and spend our money shows where our heart is (Matthew 6:21). The Proverbs also admonish us, steering us towards the middle path:

> "Two things I ask of you, O LORD;
>   do not refuse me before I die:
> Keep falsehood and lies far from me;
>   give me neither poverty nor riches,

but give me only my daily bread.
Otherwise, I may have too much and disown you
and say, 'Who is the LORD?'
Or I may become poor and steal,
and so dishonor the name of my God."
(Proverbs 30:7–9)

This is the path we need to show our children, so that they will know where true treasure is found. Here are the questions to ask:

- Are we working like dogs to finance a high standard of living? (Is it worth it?)
- Do we spend money we don't have to buy things we don't need to impress people who don't care about us anyway?
- Is my family in bondage to things?

If so, break free, scale back, get out of debt, and teach your children about the trap.

2. Impurity

Our society is increasingly promiscuous, lascivious, and sensual. The evil one knows that sensuality will lead us humans away from our Creator, Lord, and Judge. It will anesthetize us to the biblical demand for holiness (Leviticus 11:44; 1 Peter 1:15–16). Sexual impurity degrades others, reducing them to the level of objects, and makes it all but impossible for us to have real fellowship with them. That's why the Liar promotes impurity whenever he can.

What does the Bible say? Ephesians 5:3 says that impurity should not even be mentioned among us; there should not even be a hint. (For that matter, it says there shouldn't be a hint of greed, either.) Do you regularly allow your children to be exposed to impurity? And have you had honest talks with the kids about sexuality? It's much better that they hear it from us than from someone at school! And then there is the related issue of modesty:

> [23]The parts [of the body] that we think are less honorable we treat with special honor. And the parts that are unpresentable are treated with special modesty (1 Corinthians 12:23).

> [9]I also want women to dress modestly, with decency and propriety, not with braided hair or gold or pearls or expensive clothes, [10]but with good deeds, appropriate for women who profess to worship God (1 Timothy 2:9–10).

Modesty is a Christian value. Do your children dress modestly? If the answer is no, then we ought to ask ourselves, where does that influence come from? From me? From the world? And if from the world, how did it reach them?

When Peter preached his Pentecost message, he pleaded with his audience, *"Save yourselves from this corrupt generation"* (Acts 2:40). He did not urge them to save themselves from hell, though that was implied. Peter recognized the more present and immediate danger: the world itself, rebellious and lost and spinning itself into oblivion.

The world corrupts. It pollutes (James 1:27). And it wants to take up residence in your home! Are our doors and windows closed against the "men of Sodom"? (Are you sure?) Because if not, they will surely find an entrance and abuse and destroy your family.

3. Arrogance

The world exalts personal autonomy. By autonomy (literally, "self-law") we do not mean standing on one's own feet and taking responsibility for one's words and actions. That kind of autonomy is good. No, we mean denying the sovereignty of the Lord (2 Peter 2:1) and his claim on our lives, refusing to let him sit on the throne and reign over us. We want to exercise his rightful sovereignty, to rule our own lives apart from him. This is rebellion, and it is arrogance.

The Bible speaks of an entire world in rebellion against the rightful sovereignty of its Creator. According to the world, weak is the man who depends on others, confesses sin, or shows vulnerability. We want to be in charge of our lives, even though deep in our hearts we know (and dread) the fact that we don't actually have control (Jeremiah 10:23; Proverbs 14:12). We are headed for a rendezvous with destiny, and most of us would really rather not talk about it (Hebrews 2:15; Ecclesiastes 3:11; John 3:20). Those who insist on their own autonomy cannot please God.

Do our children accept instruction? Are they obedient? If they cannot obey earthly authorities, is it at all likely they will obey heavenly ones? Our insistence on governing our own lives is accompanied by arrogance and its quieter sisters, *pride* and *vanity*. Arrogance is a challenge to God's sovereignty, because it exalts self to the throne, where Jesus should be seated and ruling. "Arrogance" comes from *arrogate*, and is very similar to pride, except that pride can be subtle, whereas arrogance is usually loud and ugly. The Oxford English Dictionary defines "arrogate" as:

> To claim and assume as a right that to which one is not entitled; to appropriate without just reason, or through self-conceit, insolence, or haughtiness.

Character

Self-indulgence is the way of the world. And even when discipline does harness the self, the goal is usually self-improvement, isn't it? This is why it's so important to teach our children about character! Why all the emphasis on instructing them in the Scriptures, giving them healthy role models, and modeling character in our own lives so that they can understand the principle? It's because character means being able to say no to sin and yes to God (Titus 2:11–14). If we fail to teach them, we will not have prepared them for the world. If that is the case, sooner or later temptations will find a way into their hearts.

How Does He Do It?

The enemy launches his salvos against our hearts from three familiar bases. Here is how he barrages our souls and does all in his power to keep us attached to the world:

- *Madison Avenue* (advertising that feeds the beast, whose name is consumerism). The lie commonly takes the form, "You will be a happier person if you own product x." Moreover, an image of "caring" is concocted in the boardrooms of big business. Yet we know what is really going on. The values of big business are "Maximize profits; the ends justify the means; money is the bottom line; advertise whatever brings in revenue." Although Christians ought to offer stiff resistance to the ideology of consumerism, there is virtually none. We are rolling over and letting a whole generation be indoctrinated!

- *Hollywood* (characters who reject God's sovereignty and moral law, who model arrogance, sensuality, and violence). Infidelity and fornication are depicted as excusable, "natural" courses of action. Marital infidelity is depicted as commonplace, family dysfunction as normal. Some in the industry are intent on redefining family, discarding the Genesis plan (one man, one wife, for life). Violence, promiscuity, and materialism are glorified; and not surprisingly, injustice, crime, and hedonism follow in their wake. The slippery descent into depravity (Romans 1:18–32) is being nicely accelerated by Hollywood. Just as Noah built an ark to rescue his family from his corrupt generation (Genesis 6:5, 12–18), Christian parents have a responsibility to protect their children from the filth of the world.

- *Wall Street* (putting faith in money, the common currency of materialistic existence, rather than in Christ). Jesus noted that the Pharisees loved money, yet he assures us that what is highly valued by men is detestable in the sight of God (Luke 16:15). Trusting in money is antithetical to trusting in God. This is not to say that we should not be good stewards, invest wisely, and train our children to be financially savvy (see Chapter 21), only that we cannot put our faith in Mammon. Or governments, treaties and alliances, gated communities, or the military, for that matter. All these the Bible warns us not to trust, but rather to put our trust in the Lord.

Which of the three avenues are you and your family most vulnerable to? To which sorts of appeal (Wall Street, Hollywood, or Madison Avenue) are you most susceptible? Expect the attack to come at the weakest point.

The Solution

Jesus Christ was a realist. He taught that on this earth we will always be in "the world" (John 17:15). But that doesn't mean that we have to buy into its values. When we resist the world system, we must be prepared for stiff opposition (John 15:19).

> "I have given them Your word; and the world has hated them, because they are not of the world, even as I am not of the world. [15]I do not ask You to take them out of the world, but to keep them from the evil one. They are not of the world, even as I am not of the world. Sanctify them in the truth; Your word is truth" (John 17:14–17 NASB).

A choice must be made. We cannot change our being in the world. Even if it were possible to move to another planet, biblically speaking we would still be "in the world," since there is nowhere humans can go to escape the reach of the evil one. But we *can* decide whether to be *of* the world.

Conclusion

The dominion of darkness and the kingdom of light are starkly opposed, their respective value systems irreconcilably at odds. The world is easy to recognize: materialism, sensuality, and arrogance are blatant and rampant. But true character means being able to say no to sin and self, and yes to God and his will. These are critical elements of the worldview we must teach our children.

The next chapter will explore the primary way in which the world compromises churches, enters homes, and forces its "values" onto the hearts and minds of our children.

Television and the Media

> Finally, brothers, whatever is true, whatever is noble, whatever is right, whatever is pure, whatever is lovely, whatever is admirable—if anything is excellent or praiseworthy—think about such things (Philippians 4:8).

> But among you there must not be even a hint of sexual immorality, or of any kind of impurity, or of greed, because these are improper for God's holy people (Ephesians 5:3).

> Now the earth was corrupt in God's sight and was full of violence… So God said to Noah, "I am going to put an end to all people, for the earth is filled with violence because of them. I am surely going to destroy both them and the earth" (Genesis 6:11, 13).

As we see in the first scripture above, the Lord wants to be the Lord of our minds, sovereign over our thoughts. We are instructed to fill our minds with wholesome thoughts—"whatever is true, whatever is noble,…" In the last chapter we saw that God has called us all to a holy life, but Satan has declared war on God's values. The second scripture above reminds us of the other side of the struggle: keeping sin out of our lives. The two are complementary. The "house swept clean" of Luke 11:24–26 illustrates the point quite well. It is not enough to clean out our lives and minds of evil; we must actively seek to *replace* evil with good things.

The third scripture may be less familiar, though it shouldn't be, given the popularity of the Flood story. What moral lapse was it that "triggered" the Flood? The earth was corrupt and full of violence. Immorality is not just adultery. Why is it that Bible believers equate "immorality" with sexual sin only? Immorality is also lying. And greed. And violence. And God *hates* violence (Malachi 2:16 NRSV).

Filter!

There are many things the Lord hates and that we would do well to avoid, because they can "contaminate" our families. With respect to the areas of materialism, violence, sensuality, and other forms of immorality, we as parents will need to make some firm decisions. If we default, the decision will already have been made. Like purifying polluted water before drinking it, filtering what the media bring into the home will protect us and our children.

The Media

What do we mean by the media? We are using the word in a broader sense than just news and journalism. There are many media, both printed (books, magazines, newspapers) and visual (television, movies, the Internet, computer games). The most influential medium in our generation is still television, though the Internet is fast catching up. Nearly every American household owns at least one television set.

When I (Douglas) was little, our home had one black and white model; by the time I left for college, the number had swelled to five. When color TV came, it was all the rage, and we kids were frequently glued to the set. On it we also played Pong, a "high tech" game if ever there was one! Vicki was more "fortunate." Her family owned only one.

According to Nielsen Media Research, in 2000 the average US television was turned on more than seven hours a day, and the average American watched about four hours a day. The Kaiser Family Foundation found that in 2003, half of all US households had three or more television sets, and some 45% of parents said that if they have something important to do, they are likely to use TV to occupy their kids. This means that, on a year-round basis, most children spend more time watching television than they do in school!

Another shocking statistic has also emerged. 53% of all children's bedrooms in the United States have a television. The virtual world of the screen—and today it's no longer just the television screen—is eroding family togetherness.

And the amount of time spent with parents—those who *should* be the primary molders of their character—is only a small fraction of that spent in front of the "tube." Is this a troublesome thought? Sadly, for many parents, it is not. They have so bought into the value system of the world that they see no danger.

Today our household has one TV—and we wonder whether that is one too many! When we do watch the television, news, weather, and educational programs dominate the viewing. (Ah yes, we confess we do enjoy Wimbledon, the Australian Open, the Super Bowl, the World Series, the NCAA Basketball finals, the World Cup...) When the kids were growing up, in the summer we normally discontinued service. Since this was a time when the family was more able to be together, we did not want TV "intruding" on our time.

But most families see no problem with the TV blaring during dinnertime. A Kaiser Family Foundation Report found that in 58% of homes TV is normally on during what should be the family mealtime.

Conformed or Transformed?

The shocking thing is that TV has stepped into first place as the main shaper of our children's thoughts, conforming them to the image of the world.

> [2]Do not conform any longer to the pattern of this world, but be transformed by the renewing of your mind. Then you will be able to test and approve what God's will is—his good, pleasing and perfect will (Romans 12:2).

If *we* shouldn't be conformed to the pattern of the world, then neither should our children. If the media are enforcing conformity to the world—as we all admit they are—then why aren't Christian families more proactive? What are the character shapers of our modern generation?

This order must be pretty close to reality:

1. THE MEDIA (TV, INTERNET, MUSIC)
2. SCHOOL
3. PARENTS

But how *should* the picture look? We believe that if our biblical priorities are right, the order would be:

1. PARENTS
2. SCHOOL
3. EVERYTHING ELSE

If we are not thinking about the impact of media on our children—intentionally, conscientiously, and theologically—then we have things upside-down. So many children are worldly, drawn to the world, and becoming worldlier, and yet nothing is done to stanch the flow. What is happening in your household? Are the children conforming to the world, or being transformed by the renewing of their minds?

Watch Out!

Do the media really conspire to conform our minds to the world? Yes, they do. What are the negative effects to be guarded against?

- *Consumerism.* Commercial television is the primary medium through which consumerism is spread, convincing us and our children that we "need" many things.

- *Habituation to violence.* With all the violent images bombarding us, it is increasingly difficult to shock us and our children.

- *Sex-saturated values.* These pour into our homes through television, the Internet, and music.

- *Music.* Our children know that most MTV-style broadcasting is inappropriate for Christians to watch. Suggestive choreography, explicit or suggestive lyrics, and immodest dress draw children and adults alike to the world.

- *Family time lost.* Although it is possible to enjoy wholesome family time around television viewing, more often than not TV becomes our excuse for not talking with one another.

- *Disintegration of health.* Television has wrought great harm in its promotion of nicotine addiction, alcoholism, etc., and TV watching has been clearly linked to obesity.

- *Pathetic role models.* When convicted felons are kids' role models, we're in trouble!

- *The poor.* Despite excellent and informative documentaries, TV has also (ironically) inoculated us against caring for the poor. A few shots of poverty now and again keep its grinding reality mentally at bay. Images of the needy and of war numb our consciences. For example, the 2005 Asian tsunami disaster was publicized effectively by the media. This led to an outpouring of money, in-kind aid, concern, and prayer. But after the coverage stops, we tend to return to our insulated world. On a day-to-day basis we are numb to the plight of the poor.

- *Haunting young minds.* I will never forget the horrific scenes of violence in *The Sand Pebbles* and *In Cold Blood*, films I saw as a nine-year-old. These movies deeply affected my conscious as well as, I believe, my subconscious mind. Nor will I forget the first time I saw nudity on screen—and the (different sort of) violence that did to me. Our children's minds are so impressionable. God's word instructs us to *impress* the way of God on our children's minds (Deuteronomy 6:7). What impresses *your* children?

- *Erosion of morality.* Violence and promiscuity are highly exalted in the media, and are prime agents in our society's moral decline. The media are responsible for much of the breakdown in character so lamented by observers of the last couple of generations.

- *The church.* Many congregations, thanks to status-quo messages and worldly youth ministries, further the process of secularization and conformity to the world.

The University of the Television

Yes, TV is, for better or worse, the most influential "educational institution" of the world today. A *New York Times* survey found that the average American watches nearly five hours a day, up from the research done in 2000 mentioned above. How much are you watching? Equally important, how much do you allow your children to watch? Another good question: How much do you discuss what your children view on television? Stating there is a direct connection between television viewing and materialism is like saying there is a correlation between warfare and bloodshed. As the younger generation is fond of saying, "Duh"!

What Can I Do?

Maybe you are feeling motivated to take some action. Your situation is not our situation, but some of the ideas we share might work in your family.

- Limit television time for your children. Make sure to monitor the stations, also. Do you really want the values of our dark world to become your children's "babysitters" and "tutors"? For more mature children, restriction of TV time need not be a rule, especially once they are involved in more active and healthy pursuits.

- Block the channels you deem inappropriate. We even asked our children to help us with this, reasoning that they knew more than we did what certain programs and channels were likely to convey.

- Avoid the temptation to buy the latest and greatest high-quality television. Aren't there other ways to spend that money?

- Avoid commercials. The advertisements can be morally worse than the paid programming!

- Films—Vet movies in advance at such websites as www .screenit.com.

- Novels—What are your kids reading? You are not the "book

police," but neither should we be oblivious. We ought to be *as shrewd as snakes and as innocent as doves"* (Matthew 10:16). And discuss with them what they read.

- Magazines—The same caution is in order. Periodicals that focus on dating, sexuality, gossip, and the personal lives of the "rich and shameless" are especially damaging to Christian morals. Do you think the Lord wants your household to subscribe to them?

- The Internet—Keep the family computer in a prominent, "public" location. The children do not need to have private, unrestricted Internet access, either in their rooms or on their cell phones—this cannot be stated strongly enough! Many Christian homes follow this wise practice.

- Be radical. Improve family time by getting rid of one of its biggest disrupters and destroyers, permanently or only temporarily. Who knows? You might find that you are enjoying the extra time, the lower noise level, and the improved demeanors of your kids! As a family, do things together in lieu of television: walking, cycling, hiking, driving—activities that facilitate communication.

- Stay flexible and open. Discuss the family TV/Internet rules with your children. (Do they think they're fair? What do they see at others' homes, what do they think about it, and why?)

Is It "Our Way or the Highway"?

Not at all. In this book we offer our opinion on the media, and we are content to know that others will come to slightly different conclusions. We share our convictions and the scriptures they are based on to stimulate readers to wholesome thinking (2 Peter 3:1), not to force our opinions on anyone.

As Christians, neither we nor our children should compromise the sacred values of the Bible, no matter how much pressure the world brings to bear on us. As we follow biblical principles to the best of our understanding and ability, listen to conscience, engage in further study, seek input where needed, and make decisions about how practically to implement these principles, there are bound to be some differences of opinion.

But Isn't That Weird?

Yes, following the standards of Christ at times will appear a bit weird or eccentric to the world. But are we seeking their approval? (Galatians 1:10). As many believers began asking in the 1990s, "What would Jesus do?" That is a question each father must answer for himself, each mother for herself. Don't look to the world—or even to your church—for direction. Look to Jesus Christ. Let the Spirit and the word of God direct you, and make a decision in good faith. The Lord will honor that decision.

Conclusion

We as parents need to appreciate the enormous influence of the media if we are to *"escape the corruption in the world caused by evil desires"* (2 Peter 1:4) and enable our children to do the same. In a key scripture, Luke 17:1–3, we see that Jesus cares not only about sin, but about the media through which temptations come. We too should be concerned not so much about what's "in the air" (air pollution) as by what's "on the air." It poses the greater risk by far!

We would like to close this chapter with a memorable vignette, "The Stranger" (anonymous).

The Stranger

A few months before I was born, my dad met a stranger who was new to our small Arkansas town. From the beginning, Dad was fascinated with this enchanting newcomer, and soon invited him to live with our family. The stranger was quickly accepted and was around to welcome me into the world a few months later.

As I grew up I never questioned his place in our family. In my young mind, each member had a special niche. My parents were complementary instructors—Mom taught me to love the word of God, and Dad taught me to obey it. But the stranger was our storyteller. He could weave the most fascinating tales. Adventures, mysteries, and comedies were his daily conversations. He could hold our whole family spellbound for hours each evening. If I wanted to know about politics, history, or science, he knew it all. He knew about the past, understood the present, and seemingly could predict the future. The pictures he could draw were so lifelike that I would often laugh or cry as I watched. He was like a friend to the whole family. He took Dad and me to our first major league baseball game. He was always encouraging us to see the movies, and he even made arrangements to introduce us to several movie stars. My brother and I were deeply impressed by John Wayne in particular. The stranger was an incessant talker. Dad didn't seem to mind—but sometimes Mom would quietly get up—while the rest of us were enthralled with one of his stories of faraway places—go to her room, read her Bible, and pray.

I wonder now if she ever prayed that the stranger would leave. You see, my dad ruled our household with certain moral convictions. But this stranger never felt the obligation to honor them. Profanity, for example, was not allowed in our house—not from us, our friends, or adults. Our long-time visitor, however, used occasional four-letter words that burned my ears and made Dad squirm. To my knowledge the stranger was never confronted. My dad was a teetotaler who didn't permit alcohol in his home—not even for cooking. But the stranger felt like we needed exposure and enlightened us to other ways of life. He offered us beer and other alcoholic beverages often. He made cigarettes look tasty, cigars manly, and pipes distinguished. He talked freely (probably much too freely) about sex. His comments were sometimes blatant, sometimes suggestive, and generally embarrassing. I know now that my early concepts of the man-woman relationship were influenced by the stranger.

As I look back, I believe it was the grace of God that the stranger did not influence us more. Time after time he opposed the values of my parents. Yet he was seldom rebuked and never asked to leave. More than twelve years have passed since the stranger moved in with the young family on Morningside Drive. He is not nearly so intriguing to my Dad as he was in those early years. But if I were to walk into my living room today, you would still see him sitting over in a corner, waiting for someone to listen to him talk and watch him draw his pictures. His name?

We always just called him TV.

Healthy, Wealthy and Wise

Early to bed and early to rise
makes a man healthy, wealthy, and wise.
—Benjamin Franklin (1706–1790)

No, the famous quote is not found in the Bible. It is one of Benjamin Franklin's lines, from the 1700s. Nor by the chapter title do we mean to preach "prosperity theology"—the belief that if you put God first, you will become rich and get everything you always wanted. That theology, sadly, embodies the values of an increasing number of professing Christians. But these values are not Christian; they are diabolical. Jesus promised only food, drink, and clothing to those who sought his kingdom first—not riches (Matthew 6:25–34).

In fact, health and wealth are not always associated with righteousness in the Bible, but often with wickedness (Psalm 73:4; Habakkuk 2:6). This is not to say there aren't things we can to do improve our situation, so "healthy, wealthy, *and* wise" will form the outline for this penultimate chapter, as we conclude our discussion of Christian values.

Healthy

The human body is a remarkable thing. Well taken care of, it will normally last the better part of a century, promote a sense of well-being, and enhance our witness to Jesus Christ as we represent him in this world (2 Corinthians 2:14; 5:18–6:1). In our generation, and particularly in the developed world, health and fitness are acquiring many enemies, from the sedentary lifestyle to fast food to falling standards of physical education in the schools—all within the general malaise of self-indulgence. If you have never seen it, you should take a look at Morgan Spurlock's *Super Size Me* (2004), a film which was practically banned in many modern industrial nations through the organized opposition of the fast food restaurant chains. Mr. Spurlock ate nothing but McDonalds for thirty days, three meals a day. His health deteriorated so much that his physician told him, "You're dying." Of course the odd fast food meal won't kill you, but a lifestyle of fast food will.

What can we parents do to promote health, to keep our kids active? It begins with our theology.

> [19]Do you not know that your body is a temple of the Holy Spirit, who is in you, whom you have received from God? You are not your own; [20]you were bought at a price. Therefore honor God with your body (1 Corinthians 6:19–20).

Paul reminds us that the body is sacred, and when someone becomes a Christian, it becomes a temple. Nowhere does the Bible specify the "correct" physique. That is largely a matter of taste and culture, and the "ideal" changes from generation to generation. We must be careful not to obsess over personal appearance—ours or our children's—to the point that we buy into the worldly tenet that how you look determines your value. Paul would never have countenanced our being carried away with the body consciousness of our modern day. But he would, and did, encourage us to honor God with our bodies. That is the biblical principle.

Hopefully our children will eat well, play hard, be *reasonably* involved in sports, and take care of themselves. *"May your whole spirit, soul and body be kept blameless at the coming of our Lord Jesus Christ,"* Paul prayed (1 Thessalonians 5:23b). But one verse sometimes interpreted to say something it was never meant to say is 1 Timothy 4:8:

> [8]For bodily discipline is only of little profit, but godliness is profitable for all things, since it holds promise for the present life and *also* for the *life* to come (1 Timothy 4:8 NASB).

God here speaks about the *limited* value of physical training. The passage is not a proof text for being involved in physical activity—as if we needed one!—but an exhortation to focus on spiritual training, which is far more valuable. If we must choose between a time-consuming school sport and family devotional life, let's make the right choice.

Our philosophy is that sports should not dominate the family schedule. Our kids tended to naturally rotate through different sports. In some months, they even took a break from sports altogether. Few children are destined for sports scholarships or the world of professional athletics. Beware getting caught up in unrealistic thinking, and plowing thousands of dollars into your child's sport of choice. That can easily tear away at the family fabric—our unity and togetherness as a household.

We're not saying that it is right to ignore personal fitness in the name of God, only that our priorities must be straight. Spiritual training comes before physical training. If this is how we as parents live our lives, it will be much easier to convey this conviction to our children. Remember, they're watching us!

Wealthy

Most children are unlikely to become wealthy while still minors. But if they never learn about money, they are even more unlikely to acquire wealth after leaving home. Let's take a few minutes to talk about allowances and chores.

> [10]Whoever can be trusted with very little can also be trusted with much, and whoever is dishonest with very little will also be dishonest with much (Luke 16:10).

> [48]From everyone who has been given much, much will be demanded; and from the one who has been entrusted with much, much more will be asked (Luke 12:48b).

Is there any biblical basis for giving a child an "allowance"—a fixed amount of money, typically every week or month? Indeed there is: the scriptures above, and many more. The Lord teaches that character is built and trust is gained through small victories in small things. So, yes, there is a rationale for the practice.

We created a graduated scale, starting out at ten cents a week for a four-year-old, going up to ten dollars a week for those twelve and above. Some of you may think these allowances are on the high side, especially if you do not live in North America or Europe. (It is easy to underestimate how expensive it is to live in a developed nation.) Others may think the levels are chintzy. But kids can earn plenty of extra money through additional chores, either around the home or working for neighbors.

Whatever system you adopt, be flexible. At our house, allowances were linked to completing chores by Saturday noon. Rare were the exceptions (usually in the case of sickness or travel, but not because "Oops—I forgot!"). The system worked for our family and inculcated responsibility. Give your kids their allowances consistently. We disbursed the funds on Saturday, as soon as the weekly chores were finished. In the real world, we become used to certain financial rhythms. Childhood is a good time to acclimatize young hearts to such cycles. Allowances provide an excellent opportunity for teaching about wealth and stewardship. The Scriptures have much to say about money and our attitude towards it.

Back when our children were four, seven, and nine, we gave more serious thought to our strategy. (Not to say that we had much strategy up until that point!) Children are halfway between the total dependence of a baby and the responsibility level of an adult (2 Thessalonians 3:10). In this transitional stage, a child should be learning responsibility. We began to teach the kids to do three things with their money: *spend some, save some,* and *give some away.* Are these basic financial principles wasted on a kid? Is this a sort of "casting pearls"? Not at all! Even a child as young as four or five can begin to learn about money. And the sooner, the better. Those of us whose parents taught us about money early on have probably reaped the benefit. Yet for some reason, in many cultures talking about pecuniary matters is taboo. What a shame!

My (Douglas's) father, for example, and my grandfather were both good with money. I "absorbed" some of their financial sense, but much of what I learned came the hard way. Don't hide financial things from the kids. Rather, reveal and explain them—in age-appropriate ways, of course.

At any rate, for the kids *giving* some away was easy, since we go to church and there has never been any shortage of opportunities to give to one good cause or another.

As parents we aimed to cultivate kindness and generosity in the children. When they were younger, visiting the poor in third-world nations left an impression on them, and they have always been tenderhearted towards the needy. We had to teach them not to give *everything* away, but to have the discipline to save and (yes!) spend. Emma has donated to help needy African children. James has donated towards the church building fund. And Lily is always eager to support the adoption fund, being an adopted child herself.

Saving was also easier once we set up bank accounts for the children. (By the time our oldest was in college, all the kids had saved over $1000.) Do teach your children to save! This is a healthy habit sadly neglected by many in the grown-up world. Instead of saving money against future needs, we tend to spend money we don't have (buying on credit).

Spending, in the earlier years was more difficult. They had few wants, and we had to urge them to spend some of their money on themselves. As they grew older, they began to set their sights on objects they wanted to purchase, so persuading them to "spend some" has been become less of a challenge for us.

The older the children grow, the more they should take part in the running of the household. This is not just to alleviate the load borne by mother and father, but to prepare the kids for life on their own. Some chores are expected and must be done weekly; others are compensated. We expected the children to serve around the house as we expect Christians to serve the Lord—with a smile, not a frown. Which chores should your children do? That all depends on their ages, the household needs, your convictions on the matter, and other factors specific to your family. Perhaps your family has pets. Looking after animals is an excellent way for children to learn responsibility, and it builds confidence. As Proverbs 12:10a says, *"A righteous man cares for the needs of his animal."* In a small way, it is also preparation for parenthood—though we would not want to press the analogies between pets and children too far!

Whatever you decide, aim for moderation: not too many chores, not too few. Consistency and a positive atmosphere are important. Work should be seen, and experienced, in a spiritual and joyous light, not a legalistic and onerous one.

Wise

Wisdom is primarily a spiritual quality in the Bible (Proverbs 1:1–7). It is not the same thing as knowledge. There are some highly educated people in this world who are not wise according to God's standard, and there are many who have never finished school who are wise in Christ. Someone defined an intellectual as "someone educated beyond his intelligence." The definition may be a bit unfair, but it points out the vanity and pride that may accompany much learning. Having said that, since God's word does emphasize glorifying God with our *minds*, it is fair to ask whether we as parents are using the many tools at our disposal which can help our children do just that. Jesus repeated the "greatest commandment" in this way: *Love the Lord your God with all your heart and with all your soul and with all your mind* (Matthew 22:37).

Loving God with our minds involves thinking, reflection, questioning, and mental growth. One of the seven or eight terms for a Christian in the New Testament is "disciple," which means a *student* or *learner*. All Christians are to continue to grow in their knowledge of the Lord and his word (2 Timothy 2:15).

It is much harder to love God and feel close to him if you cannot read. In past generations, people were better listeners. Private ownership of books (apart from churches and the rich) was virtually unheard of until after the printing press brought books within the economic reach of the upper middle class. In biblical times, it is safe to say that virtually no one owned a Bible, apart from the king (Deuteronomy 17:18–19) and the synagogue or church (Acts 17:10–12). That explains why we do not find scriptures explicitly telling us to "read the Bible." Not everyone could afford books, but people could and did pay attention to what they heard.

Today, if you are reading this book, you almost certainly also have access to a Bible. Read it well! An anti-intellectual attitude on our part does not help our children. It only reinforces that in many juvenile circles it is considered "uncool" to be smart or to enjoy school.

But is this right? God is intelligent, beyond our wildest imagination. Jesus Christ was supremely smart, even though you do not often hear sermons about that quality. People were amazed at how much he knew, even though he had never attended *their* schools (John 7:15–16). The thrust of the passage is easily missed. It is not emphasizing how *little* Jesus knew, but how *much* he knew! There is no excuse to be found here for a careless approach to Bible study or a refusal to think theologically. In the old days, the preacher was often the most educated person in his town, and preaching served to educate the parish.

Parents, let's encourage our children to love school. Work with your children's teachers. As we all know from our own experience, a great teacher can make a lifelong impact on your child.

Play games with your children. This will expand their minds far beyond the point to which most television channels will take them.

Local libraries and bookstores also appeal to many children, especially if they come from a reading family. Let's avail ourselves of the many easily accessible resources to help our children enjoy learning, develop mentally, and ultimately aspire to love the Lord their God with all their mind.

Show them scriptures that will inspire them. Daniel 1 describes the four Hebrew exiles brought to Babylon (modern day Iraq) to serve the Babylonian government:

> [4]…young men…showing aptitude for every kind of learning, well informed, quick to understand… He was to teach them the language and literature of the Babylonians… [17]To these four

> young men God gave knowledge and understanding of all kinds
> of literature and learning (Daniel 1:4, 17).

These men were smart, alert, and willing to push themselves. Their young minds were supple: they were ready to learn not only a new language, but its literature as well.

Encourage your children to read! If they see you reading, they will tend to follow in your footsteps. If the parents have a learner's spirit, it will rub off on the children. As someone quipped, "The man who does not read good books has no advantage over the man who cannot read them."

What Bible do your children read? If they are good readers and can handle the NIV, TNIV (gauged to a 13½-year-old reading level), or the HCSB, good for them. Younger kids—and even some older ones—will benefit from simpler translations, like the New Century Version or Today's English Version (Good News for Modern Man). Our favorite for preteens is the *Adventure Bible Handbook,* which is based on the NIV but is full of pictures and other interesting graphics. Most teens would probably like it!

Don't let education, and the wonderful gift of literacy, be wasted. The benefits of education are many. Your children will be more confident, secure better jobs, be better citizens, and be more able to provide for their own families. But beyond all these important considerations, they'll be equipped to engage the Lord their God *mentally*—with all their mind.

We close this chapter with these words of encouragement:

- Get your children reading. This will open many doors, especially doors of the mind.

- Help them to read and understand the Bible. This will open the door into the "mind of Christ" (1 Corinthians 2:16).

- Help them to enjoy and finish school. These should be happy years, and the skills learned in school will serve them for the rest of their lives.

- Get them to go beyond school, to college, if possible. And make sure they finish their university studies. Dropping out is a character issue, and a degree will open many more doors.

This concludes Section VI. We have explored what the Bible says about Family, Parents, Children, Rhythms, and Values. In our conclusion, which is the final chapter, we will share with you the true story of the Three Little Pigs.

VII

Conclusion and Resources

The Three Little Pigs

By the breath of God ice is given, and the broad waters are frozen fast (Job 37:10 NRSV).

Our skin has been blackened as though baked in an oven (Lamentations 5:10b NLT).

"Some ferocious animal has devoured him. He has surely been torn to pieces" (Genesis 37:33b).

Once upon a time a family tried their hand at raising guinea pigs. The three little pigs were named Copper, Midnight, and Twilight, and they were all very cute and fluffy. The following is a true tale, though we wish it weren't. You see, what happened wasn't intentional. We were honestly unaware of the dangers. And they were so dependent on us!

Bitter Cold

The first little pig slept in the garage, in its cage. We did not realize that during our weekend trip the temperature would fall to 5°F (-15°C). After all, it was November. But this was a freak cold snap. Besides, *Cavia porcellus*, the South American rodent-like animal and popular pet, is well endowed with fur. It never occurred to us that there was any risk, otherwise we would have brought her into the house. And in fact there was no danger, except for the fact that the side door had accidentally been left open, allowing the freezing air to come into the garage.

Two days later, as we pulled into our driveway that frigid

Monday morning and opened the garage, we could see Copper (piggy number one) pressed into a corner of the cage. She looked misshapen, gaunt. Vicki exclaimed, "Copper's dead!"

I replied, "Well, hold on, maybe she survived—even though it doesn't look too good."

"The pig's dead," Vicki repeated. Sure enough, the guinea pig was not only dead, but frozen fast. (Yes, the chapter's introductory scriptures do tie in to the plot of the story.)

The ground was too hard to dig a hole in, so I put the carcass in the most logical place (logical to a man's way of thinking). When my daughter Emma came home from school—she was quite young at the time—we told her that Copper had died of cold. (Or was it "a cold"?) Of course I did not confess that I was guilty of third-degree porcicide.

After the tears, Emma asked me, "Where is Copper now? Did you bury her, Daddy?"

When I hesitated, Emma burst out, "You didn't!" Woman's intuition—she correctly guessed that I had simply wrapped her stiff body and laid her to rest in the rubbish bin, as the trash collectors were coming that day. Ah, but that is only one little piggy.

Blazing Heat

The following summer was a hot one in Washington DC. The evening of July 4th was pleasant enough, so I had carried the guinea pig cage outside and set it on the grass. Midnight (piggy number two) always loved munching the green grass, and I saw no problem leaving the cage outside. But the next day temperatures soared to 100°F (38°C). I remembered the cage by late morning. (Or was it our youngest, Lily, reminding me? She has an excellent memory.) By that time he was already *in extremis,* panting, hyperventilating, desperately grabbing for air. It didn't help that his fur coat was jet black—the optimal color for absorbing sunlight. (That's why we called him Midnight.)

Lily and I carried his limp body into the garage and tried to cool him down by plunging him into a bucket of cool water. The baptismal approach failed. So I brought him into the kitchen, into the air conditioned house, surely a better environment for recovery. There I tried to get some drops of watermelon juice into his mouth through a straw.

"Maybe this will help the little fellow perk up," I thought to myself. But Midnight still had trouble breathing. I couldn't perform mouth-to-mouth, since the pig was only 10 inches (25 cm) long. But I did press down on his rib cage, trying to assist the pig's labored breathing. After thirty minutes of gasps and spasms—the inevitable. It stretched out all four legs, made one last gasp, and gave up the ghost. (If you are a veterinarian reading this, please do not report me!)

Once again I had to break the news to Emma, who was in Florida. On the way home from collecting her at the airport, I didn't know how to begin the doleful tale. "You know, this was a really hot week..."

"Yes, Daddy?"

"Well, I'm afraid I have some bad news for you. You know how dark colors absorb sunlight, making whatever is dark become hotter and hotter? Especially with so much dark fur, er—." Sobs were coming from my daughter.

"Not Midnight, Daddy!" (intense sobbing)

"Yes, it's Midnight."

When she had composed herself, Emma inquired, "How come every time I go away, one of the pigs dies? So, where is he?"

"In the back garden. I'll show you where when we get home." (At least this time I was ceremonious enough to give it a proper burial.)

But, yes, that's only two little piggies. Number three was called Sunlight.

Predator

A year later Sunlight was sleeping out on the patio, in her protective cage. The door was (presumably) latched shut. Who forgot to secure the cage door, I do not know. But the next morning before breakfast Vicki called out, with total solemnity, "Doug, *bad* news. The pig has been eaten. It's really ugly; I don't think we should let the girls see it."

Sure enough, the cage had been opened—we think by a raccoon, which is a clever animal—and several parts of the pig had been mauled. The little critter had no chance. Guinea pigs are not particularly fierce, if you've ever seen one. In fact, I think it's amazing they've survived on the earth as long as they have. Anyway, I'd never seen the *inside* of a guinea pig before. I know you're wondering if I felt guilty. Yes, perhaps a twinge of guilt, a pang. One killed by the cold, another by the heat, yet another by a wild animal.

Not surprisingly, no family has asked me to look after their guinea pigs since then—trust is lost so quickly!—until this weekend. As I type these very words, we are looking after one more *Cavia* for a neighbor. It's *inside* the house, in a cage (locked against our curious cats), and it is doing just fine, I hear. (I haven't dared even take a peek.)

Live and Learn

Of course now that we are better informed—notice how I shifted from "I" to "we," bringing my wife into it now?—now that we are profoundly educated in the ins and outs of bringing up *Cavia porcellus*, we know all about what it takes, including how to prevent them from dying unnecessarily. As for the future, would we have any excuse if one froze to death? Or baked to death in the summer heat, or was savaged by a wild animal? No, we would be without excuse. As Jesus said, *"If I had not come and spoken to them, they would not be guilty of sin. Now, however, they have no excuse for their sin"* (John 15:22).

The moral of this tale is that the Lord expects us not only to live, but to learn. Even though the three little pigs all died accidentally, we had flouted some rather basic biological principles. We were guilty of neglect. Never again!

Okay, such things "happen." But then so do things "happen" to our children. They may be affected by the bitter cold of unbelief, ubiquitous in academic environments hostile to Christian faith. Or the heat of sin and sensuality can send them into a downward spiral of worldliness. Have we adequately protected them? And what about the predators—those in the world, including cyberspace—who would gladly make our dear children into objects, addicts, or criminals? Are there any "doors" open that should not be? The world is a hostile place, especially for children.

Three "Ns"

Having now studied what God says about the matter, we are sure you as parents want to do the right thing. After all, our children are more precious than *Cavia porcellus* (Matthew 10:31). Where are you coming from? What has been your situation up till now?

- *Neglect.* In the past you may have neglected to carefully follow the word of God. You may have sought little advice and read few parenting books, but now you are seriously studying biblical parenting principles for yourself. You are determined to change. Don't worry—the Bible will direct you where to focus. Let God's priorities be your priorities, and you will not go wrong. We don't want to be guilty of focusing on minor issues while major ones go unaddressed (Matthew 23:23).

- *Nonchalance.* Some parents are so uninvolved with their kids—so "hands off"—that they have little idea what the real issues are. Maybe this is because they immersed themselves in careerism. Or perhaps they felt inadequate to parent, and so closed their eyes, "shut down," and prayed for the best. But nonchalance is not an acceptable attitude. If we've been uninvolved or distant, we need to repent. Our children deeply need us—and not just when they are little and helpless. What should our attitude be? What is the attitude of our heavenly Father towards us?

- *Naivety.* Perhaps you simply underestimated the perils—the influence of the world, the corrupting power of the media, our call to be *separate* from the world, or the crucial need to instruct our children. If so, you have been naïve. We are all naïve about some things, but we can learn. Become wise through the word of God (Proverbs 1:2–5).

Unless the Lord Builds the House...

Let us return to the animals for a moment. We did better with pets after those days. We have had cats, a dog, and even fish in a small pond dug by the family. We have been casualty-free for a number of years. (Well, maybe a couple of fish.) We're learning.

Raising kids is a bit different from raising pets. It's a thousand times harder! And unspeakably more important in the Lord's eyes. To succeed, we need the Lord on our side. We need his guidance, his parenting principles inscribed on our hearts. It is time for a psalm, as we return to the Bible passage with which we began our study:

> *¹A Song of Ascents. Of Solomon.*
>
> Unless the LORD builds the house,
>> those who build it labor in vain.
> Unless the LORD guards the city,
>> the guard keeps watch in vain.
> ²It is in vain that you rise up early
>> and go late to rest,
> eating the bread of anxious toil;
>> for he gives sleep to his beloved.
> ³Sons are indeed a heritage from the LORD,
>> the fruit of the womb a reward.
> ⁴Like arrows in the hand of a warrior
>> are the sons of one's youth.
> ⁵Happy is the man who has
>> his quiver full of them.
> He shall not be put to shame
>> when he speaks with his enemies in the gate.
>>   (Psalm 127:1 NRSV)

This short psalm reminds us that the Lord wants to be involved in the building of our house (home), and his blessing is meant to reach many generations of our offspring. Moreover, though bringing up sons and daughters is hard work, it is a lot lighter work when we follow God's principles. (Just like following Christ—Matthew 11:30; 1 John 5:3.) We can sleep easy when we're being taught by our heavenly Father, who is the ideal parent. Finally, the psalm reminds us that children are a tremendous blessing.

Let us love those children the way the Lord wants us to. Because before we know it, they will be launched.

Parenting Resources

Books, Magazines and Websites

BOOKS

Bach, David. *Automatic Millionaire*. New York: Broadway, 2004, ISBN 0-7679-1410-4.

Blomberg, Craig L. *Neither Poverty nor Riches: A Biblical Theology of Material Possessions*. Grand Rapids: Eerdmans, 1999. ISBN 0-8308-2607-6.

Boger, Lee. *But What About the Children?* Livermore, California: Bookshelf Press, 2005. ISBN 1-59594-008-1.

Boteach, Shmuley, *Shalom in the Home: Smart Advice for a Peaceful Life*. Des Moines: Meredith Books, 2007, ISBN 978-0-696-23507-8.

Brodzinsky, David M, Marshal D. Schechter, and Robin Marantz Henig. *Being Adopted: The Lifelong Search for Self*. New York: Random House, 1992. ISBN 0-385-41426-9.

Campbell, Ross. *How to Really Love Your Teen*. Colorado Springs: Cook Communications, 2004. ISBN 0-7814-3913-2.

Chapman, Gary and Ross Campbell. *The Five Love Languages of Children*. Chicago: Northfield, 1997. ISBN 1-881273-65-2.

Cloud, Henry and John Townsend. *Boundaries*. Grand Rapids: Zondervan, 1992. ISBN 0-310-24745-4.

_____. *Boundaries with Kids.* Grand Rapids: Zondervan, 2001. ISBN 0310243157.

Dobson, James. *Love Must Be Tough: New Hope for Families in Crisis.* Dallas: Word, 1996. ISBN 0-8499-1341-1.

_____. *The New Dare to Discipline.* Carol Stream, Ill.: Tyndale, 1996. ISBN 0-8423-0506-8.

_____. *The New Hide or Seek: Building Self-Esteem in Your Child.* Grand Rapids: Baker, 2001. ISBN 0-8007-5680-0.

_____. *The New Strong-Willed Child.* Carol Stream, Ill.: Tyndale, 2001. ISBN 0842336222.

_____. *Parenting Isn't for Cowards.* Dallas: Word, 1987. ISBN 0-8499-40140-1.

_____ and Gary Bauer. *Children at Risk.* Dallas: Word, 1990. ISBN 084-9935-849.

Evans, Debra. *Kindred Hearts: Nurturing the Bond between Mother and Daughter.* Wheaton: Tyndale, 1997. ISBN: 1-5617-9437-6.

Everson, Eva Marie and Jessica Everson. *Sex, Lies, and the Media: What Your Kids Know and Aren't Telling You.* Life Journey. ISBN 6781441951.

Farrar, Steve, King *Me: What Every Son Wants and Needs from His Father.* Chicago: Moody Publishers, 2005. ISBN 0-8024-3319-7.

Faulkner, Paul. *Raising Faithful Kids in a Fast-Paced World.* West Monroe, Louisiana: Howard, 1995. ISBN 1-878990-52-7.

Getz, Gene. *Rich in Every Way: Everything God Says about Money and Possessions.* West Monroe, Louisiana: Howard, 2004. ISBN 1-5822-9390-2.

Goleman, Daniel. *Emotional Intelligence: Why It Can Matter More than IQ.* New York: Bantam, 1995), ISBN 0-553-37506-7.

Huggins, Kevin. *Parenting Adolescents: A Biblical Model for Parents.* Colorado Springs, Navpress, 1989. ISBN 0891096973.

Hunter, Lynda. *A Comprehensive Guide to Parenting on Your Own.* Grand Rapids: Zondervan, 1997. ISBN 0-310-21309-6.

Laing, Sam and Geri. *Raising Awesome Kids in Troubled Times.* Spring, TX: Illumination Publishers, 2017. ISBN 978-1-946800-66-4.

_____. *The Essential 8: Principles of a Strong Family.* Spring, TX: Illumination Publishers, 2013. ISBN 1939086132.

_____ and Elizabeth Laing Thompson. *The Wonder Years: Parenting Preteens & Teens.* Billerica, Mass.: DPI, 2001. ISBN 157782599.

Lewis, Paul. *40 Ways to Teach Your Child Values.* Grand Rapids: Zondervan, 1997. ISBN 0-3102-1699-0.

Louis, John and Karen. *Good Enough Parenting.* Spring, TX:, Illumination Publishers, 2015. ISBN 978-1-939086-84-6.

The One Year Book of Devotions for Kids #1. Wheaton: Tyndale, 1993. ISBN 084235087X.

The One Year Book of Devotions for Kids #2. Wheaton: Tyndale, 1995. ISBN 0842345922.

The One Year Book of Devotions for Kids #3. Wheaton: Tyndale, 1997. ISBN 0842346627.

Ramsey, David. *Financial Peace Revisited.* New York: Viking, 2003, ISBN 0-670-03208-5.s

Rosemond, John. *Teen-Proofing: Fostering Responsible Decision Making in Your Teenager.* Kansas City: Andrews McMeel Publishing, 2001. ISBN 978-0-7407-1021-6.

Scazzero, Peter. *The Emotionally Healthy Church.* Grand Rapids: Zondervan, 2003), ISBN 0-310-24654-7.

Schlesinger, Laura. *Parenthood by Proxy: Don't Have Them If You Won't Raise Them.* New York: HarperCollins, 2000. ISBN 0-06-019125-2.
Schlosser, Eric. *Fast Food Nation: The Dark Side of the All-American Meal.* San Francisco: Harper Collins, 2002. ISBN 0-395-97789-4.

Sheldon, Charles M. *In His Steps.* New York: Smithmark, 1992, ISBN 0-8317-4973-3.

Sider, Ronald J. *Rich Christians Living in an Age of Hunger: Moving from Affluence to Generosity.* Nashville: Word, 1997. ISBN 0-8499-1424-8.

Smalley, Gary. *The Key to Your Child's Heart.* Dallas: Word, 1992. ISBN 0-8499-0947-3.

Stinnett, Nick and Nancy, and Joe and Alice Beam. *Fantastic Families: 6 Proven Steps to Building a Strong Family.* New York: Howard Books, 1999. ISBN 1-58229-080-6.

Tripp, Paul David. *Age of Opportunity: A Biblical Guide to Parenting Teens.* Phillipsburg, NJ: P&R, 1997. ISBN 0-8755-2605-5.

Tripp, Tedd. *Shepherding a Child's Heart.* Wapwallopen, PA: Shepherd Press, 1995. ISBN 0-9663786-0-1.

Verrier, Nancy. *The Primal Wound: Understanding the Adopted Child.* Lafayette, California: Nancy Verrier, 1993. ISBN 0-9636480-0-4.

Wilkinson, Bruce H. *Family Walk: 52 Weekly Devotions for Your Family.* Grand Rapids: Zondervan, 1991. ISBN 0-310-54241-3.

Wuthnow, Robert. *Poor Richard's Principle: Recovering the American Dream Through the Moral Dimension of Work, Business, & Money* (Princeton: Princeton University Press, 1996), ISBN 0-691-02892-3.

Ziegler, Tom and Lori. *As For Me and My House: 50 Easy-to-Use Devotionals for Families.* Spring, TX: Illumination Publishers, 2003. ISBN 1-5778-2187-4.

FOR BLENDED FAMILIES: Books

Deal, Ron. L. *The Smart Stepfamily: 7 Steps to a Healthy Family* (rev. ed.) Bethany House, 2014.

Debrincat, Gina. *Matrix of the Blended Family.* Word Alive Press, 2010.

Houpe, Steve and Donna. *Becoming One Family: Bringing Blended Families Together.* Tulsa: Harrison House, 2008.

Marsolini, Maxine. *Raising Children in Blended Families: Helpful Insights, Expert Opinions, and True Stories.* Kregel, 2006.

Patty, Sandi. *Life in the Blender: Blending Families, Lives, and Relationships with Grace.* Thomas Nelson, 2009.

Petherbridge, Laura. *101 Tips for the Smart Stepmom: Expert Advice from One Stepmom to Another.* Bethany House, 2014.

Websites

- http://www.whatchristianswanttoknow.com/christian-advice-for-blended-families-7-helpful-tips/
- https://www.gotquestions.org/blended-families.html
- http://www.whatchristianswanttoknow.com/does-the-bible-discuss-blended-families-a-christian-study/
- http://www.focusonthefamily.com/marriage/marriage-challenges/remarriage-and-blended-families/the-smart-blended-marriage
- https://www.2equal1.com/advice/biblical-foundations-for-blended-families/

CHILDREN'S MAGAZINES

American Girl Magazine
Ages: 8–11 years
Pleasant Company Publications
6 issues per year

Dig Magazine
Ages: 8–14 years
Archaeological Institute of America
9 issues per year

Biography Today Series
Ages: 9 years and up
Omnigraphics, Inc.
3 issues per year

Discovery Girls
Ages: 8–12 years
Discovery Girls
6 issues per year

Dream/Girl:
The Arts Magazine for Girls
Ages: 9–14 years
Dowell Media
6 issues per year

Footsteps
Ages: 9 years and up
Cobblestone Publishing Company
5 issues per year

Kids Discover
Ages: 6 and up
Discovery Kids
12 issues per year

Muse
Ages: 10 years and up
Carus Publishing Company
9 issues per year

National Geographic for Kids
Ages: 8 years and up
National Geographic Society
10 issues per year

New Moon Girls Magazine
Ages: 8–14 years
New Moon Publishing, Inc.
6 issues per year

Purple Mountain Press
Ages: 9–12 years
Purple Mountain Press
24 issues per year

Ranger Rick Jr.
Ages: 4–7 years
National Wildlife Federation
10 issues per year

Stone Soup
Ages: 8–13 years
Children's Art Foundation
6 issues per year

Youthline USA
Ages: 8–14 years
Youthline USA
48 issues per year

Zoobooks
Ages: 4–11 years
Wildlife Education Ltd.
10 issues per year

USEFUL WEBSITES FOR PARENTS & TEACHERS

http://www.aacc.net
Website of the American Association of Christian Counselors. Applications of biblical counseling principles to family relationships.

http://www.barna.org
Homepage for The Barna Group. Well-thought-through and factually substantiated resources relating to families and much more.

http://www.family.org
While you and I may not agree with everything James Dobson teaches, most of our readers will agree with most of it. His website is the official site of Focus on the Family.

http://familydoctor.org
From the American Academy of Family Physicians, this site offers health information for the whole family.

www.familydnyamics.net
The website of the Family Dynamics Institute. Changes in the marriage inevitably lead to changes in family dynamics; everyone wins.

http://www.familylife.com
Family Life contains a wide array of material on marriage, parenting, singles, and life issues.

http://endsexualexploitation.org/
The National Center on Sexual Exploitation is a nonprofit organization that, among other things, works through constitutional means to curb illegal traffic in obscenity and uphold standards of decency in media.

http://screenit.com
A helpful website for reviewing movies and music, new or old. Categories rated include alcohol/drugs, blood/gore, disrespect/bad attitude, frightening/tense scenes, guns/weapons, music, profanity, sex/nudity, smoking, and violence.

http://www.teachingvalues.com
One of the most extensive sources on the web for parents, teachers, and anyone involved with character education for children.

For all the latest news, articles and insights
from the ministry of Douglas Jacoby go to:
www.DouglasJacoby.com

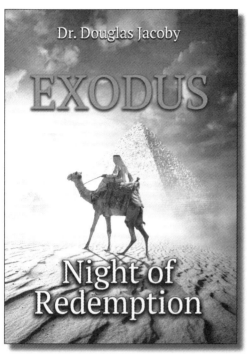

Books
by
Douglas
Jacoby

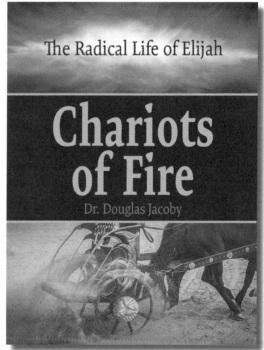

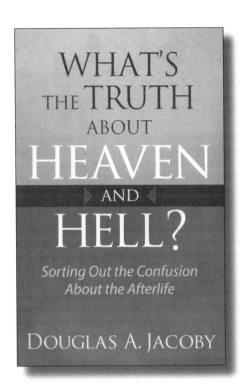

WHAT'S THE TRUTH ABOUT HEAVEN AND HELL?

Sorting Out the Confusion
About the Afterlife

DOUGLAS A. JACOBY

THRIVE!
Using Psalms to Help You Flourish

DOUGLAS JACOBY

Books
by
Douglas
Jacoby

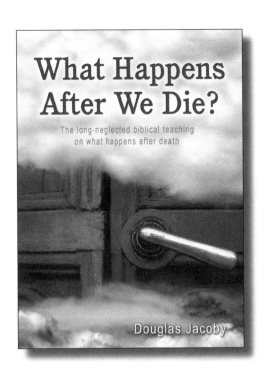

What Happens
After We Die?

The long-neglected biblical teaching
on what happens after death

Douglas Jacoby

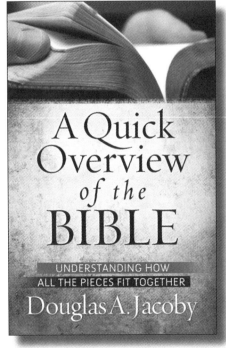

A Quick
Overview
of the
BIBLE

UNDERSTANDING HOW
ALL THE PIECES FIT TOGETHER

Douglas A. Jacoby

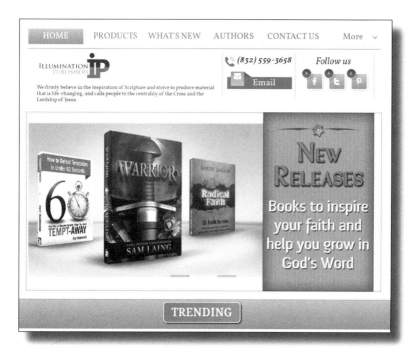